LEARNER DRIVER

D0831105

An associated David & Charles title
SENSIBLE DRIVING
The Logical Basis of Everyday Motoring
By M. J. Hosken

LEARNER DRIVER

Joseph Kells

DAVID & CHARLES

NEWTON ABBOT   LONDON   NORTH POMFRET (VT)   VANCOUVER

Acknowledgements

The publishers and author wish to offer their sincere thanks to the following for assistance given, and diagrams supplied:
The Department of the Environment
The Royal Automobile Club which examines and registers driving instructors, issues competition licences, organises the 'L Driver of the Year Competition', and is the governing body for motor sport in Great Britain
The Austin Morris Group of British Leyland Ltd, Longbridge
The Car and Motorcycle Drivers' Association
The Institute of Advanced Motorists
The League of Safe Drivers

ISBN 0 7153 6794 3

Library of Congress Catalog Card Number 74–81073

© Joseph Kells 1975

Set in 11 on 13pt Linotype Baskerville and printed in Great Britain by Latimer Trend & Company Ltd Plymouth for David & Charles (Holdings) Limited South Devon House   Newton Abbot   Devon

Published in the United States of America by David & Charles Inc North Pomfret   Vermont 05053 USA

Published in Canada by Douglas David & Charles Limited 132 Philip Avenue   North Vancouver   BC

Contents

CHAPTER ONE

Driving Preliminaries

Before attempting to drive a car on public roads it is essential to comply with the legal requirements as regards document-ation. This means you must make sure that:

(i) The vehicle you are to drive is properly licensed (if the vehicle is a driving-school car, then it is the duty of the school to attend to this).

(ii) Your insurance is in order, ie, that it covers the liabilities in respect of at least third-party risks to yourself and to any other person who might drive the vehicle. (Again, if a school car, then the school is primarily responsible for this.)

(iii) There is in force a current Department of the Environment (DoE) Test Certificate for the vehicle if it is over the prescribed age limit. (Once more, the driving school's liability if it is a school car.)

In addition to the above, a learner driver should hold a provisional driving licence valid for the class of vehicle he intends to drive and should ensure that his eyesight is up to the standard required for the Driving Test.

If you are wise, you will have enrolled with a reputable driving school. Now that all instructors are required to be approved by the Department of the Environment it is by no means as easy to go wrong as it was some years ago. Remember, however, that when you are selecting an instructor you are choosing someone to entrust with your training in basic driving skills and also in roadcraft. If you were, instead, seeking a firm of engineers with whom to entrust the repair of a valuable colour television set, you would undoubtedly make careful enquiries and eventually decide upon the one which appeared to possess the most highly qualified technicians and had acquired a reputation for efficiency. Now it is your entire driving career which is at stake—more than that, your life, those of your family, and those who are around you on the road all the time you are at the wheel of a car. It is, therefore, doubly important for you to select an instructor in whom you have confidence right from the very first lesson.

Obviously there are instructors who are content to obtain the minimum qualifications called for by law, ie the Department of the Environment's Certificate of Approval as a Driving Instructor. Those who are really interested in their work and who enjoy teaching are, just as obviously, more likely to possess certain additional qualifications, such as that of Royal Automobile Club Registered Driving Instructor, or Motor Schools Association Approved Driving Instructor. Such instructors are easily recognised, for they are proud to display on their vehicles their additional qualifications. Indeed, many of those who possess such qualifications prefer to display them instead of the DoE plates alone.

This book cannot replace a good instructor, for he will be able to analyse your faults in driving and explain how they can be overcome. It can, however, assist you a great deal by augmenting the explanations given you in the car, and by affording you an opportunity for revision of certain items before your next lesson on the road. Sometimes, too, you may find a point explained in a slightly different manner to that used by your instructor. Both methods will certainly be correct, but a point explained in another way or from a fresh angle may assist you to understand something you were finding difficult.

EYESIGHT

The eyesight test is an extremely simple one. It consists of reading a standard car numberplate at a distance of 75ft, and your instructor will no doubt satisfy himself that you are able to do this before permitting you to drive a car on a public road. If you normally wear spectacles, then it is an offence to drive without them. When you have satisfied your instructor concerning your eyesight, you will have already passed one part of the driving test.

THE HIGHWAY CODE

Section 74 of the Road Traffic Act says that a failure on the part of a person to observe a provision of the Highway Code shall not in itself render that person liable to criminal proceedings of any kind, but that any such failure may, in any proceedings (whether criminal or civil, and including proceedings for an offence under the Act) be relied upon by any party to the proceedings as tending to establish or to negative any liability which is in question in those proceedings.

Which means, of course, that the better one knows one's Highway Code, the less likely one is to get into trouble whilst driving under normal circumstances.

There are several sections in the Highway Code booklet, and it is advisable to first read the general ones which deal with what pedestrians should do, how cyclists should behave and so on. After all, the more you know about how they *should* behave, the more intelligently you will be able to anticipate their actions when you are behind the wheel. One salient point about both pedestrians and cyclists is that the most unpredictable, and therefore the most dangerous to you as a driver (and to themselves, of course), are the very young and the very old. These should always be given plenty of room and approached or overtaken cautiously.

Now for the portions of the Code which will apply to you as a motorist. It is quite certain that your instructor will not have the slightest intention of letting you loose on roundabouts, traffic lights, busy shopping centres and so on until after quite a few lessons, so at this stage you will be perfectly safe in concentrating on the things you know he will ask you to do, such as moving off, keeping to the left, pulling in and stopping. This business of stopping means, of course, that you do not just have to know HOW to stop, but also where NOT to stop or park your car, so make sure that you have read all about what he is likely to do on any particular lesson well before it takes place. You will then lighten his work and enable him to concentrate on more important matters, such as the actual technique of handling the controls. If half the lesson is spent pulled in at the side of the road discussing the dos and don'ts of the Code, then half your expensive lesson is wasted.

INTRODUCTION TO THE CAR

The first thing to which attention should be paid is one's seating position. Your instructor will explain how the seat is adjusted in your car and it is most important that you should be absolutely comfortable all the time you are driving, and whether the car is going forwards or backwards. If your height is above or below average, your instructor will know how to compensate for this and will advise you about such things as cushions (very bad, because they are apt to slide around at critical moments), blocks under the seat-runners, and so on. When you at last think you have achieved a perfectly comfortable seating position, try to push the clutch pedal (the extreme left-hand one) right down to the floor. If you are unable to do this without stretching, then your position is not yet right. On the other hand, you should be able to do it without finding yourself squashed against the steering wheel. Try to reach all the controls. When you are able to do so with ease then you have the correct position.

Now, sitting quite naturally and without craning your head in any way, look into the rear-view mirror in the centre of the upper portion of the windscreen. You should be able to see straight through the middle of the back window. If it is necessary to adjust this, remember two points: (i) When adjusting the mirror, hold it by the edges so as not to smear the glass with your fingers, and (ii) try to keep your head in the position it will be whilst driving along.

THE ESSENTIAL CONTROLS

The accelerator is the extreme right-hand pedal and governs the speed of the engine. (See Figure 1.) When your instructor calls for 'more gas' or 'more revs', he means you to press this pedal harder. Novice drivers tend to go from one extreme to the other, mainly because they are trying to do so many things at once that they forget to listen to the engine. Try to acquire the habit of missing nothing—not even the song of your engine. Once you really became accustomed to it you will become conscious of the slightest irregularity and this will serve as an early warning of impending trouble. This is a habit which can perhaps save you a great deal of money.

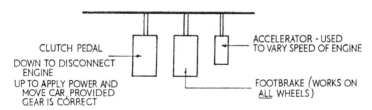

CLUTCH PEDAL
DOWN TO DISCONNECT ENGINE
UP TO APPLY POWER AND MOVE CAR, PROVIDED GEAR IS CORRECT

ACCELERATOR - USED TO VARY SPEED OF ENGINE

FOOTBRAKE (WORKS ON ALL WHEELS)

Figure 1   Layout of pedal controls on a conventional car

The footbrake is the centre one of the three pedals. It acts upon all four wheels, and is quite powerful. It is therefore the brake to use in normal driving for slowing or stopping the car. Note that if the car pulls to one side or the other when this brake is applied, then obviously the brakes are out of adjustment.

The clutch is the left-hand pedal. Its purpose is to connect or disconnect engine and gearbox. In the 'down' position it disconnects the engine, and in the 'up' position (which it normally is) it connects the engine and so applies 'drive' to the car. The clutch acts in conjunction with the gears, as will be explained in greater detail later.

The gear lever. Reference to Figure 2 will show you the layout of gears applicable to your particular make of car. Reverse gear is usually selected by either lifting the lever or knocking it past a detent spring. This is a built-in safety device to prevent selection of reverse gear in normal forward driving, which would cause serious damage to the gearbox.

In general, the reason for having a selection of gears is to afford the engine a greater degree of flexibility than would otherwise be possible. If you have ever tried to push a car, you will know that it takes a great deal more energy to start it moving than it does to keep it rolling. This is why we have a low gear which is designed to transmit a great deal of power for moving off from rest, climbing very steep hills and so on. The main points to bear in mind when learning about the use of gears are these: *The lower the gear, the lower the speed but the greater the power,* and *the higher the gear, the higher the speed but the lower the power.*

Hence we can conveniently regard first (or bottom) gear as the workhorse of the gears. Like a plough-horse, it is all brute force and muscle, but possesses little speed. The next gear up provides somewhat more speed but less power, and so on until we reach top gear, which provides the maximum speed of which the car is capable but at the same time has the least reserve of power. (This is why a driver has to change down to lower gear[s] when the car is climbing a hill.)

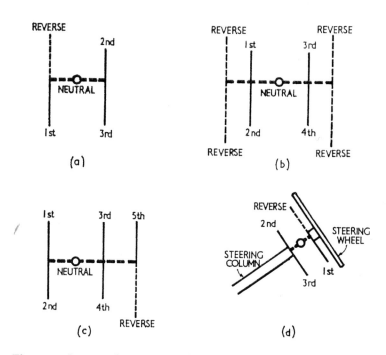

Figure 2 Layout of gears on various types of car: (a) usual arrangement for 3-gear car, though position of reverse may vary; (b) in a 4-gear box, reverse may be in any of the positions shown; (c) standard layout for 5-gear cars; (d) arrangement for a 3-speed column gearchange

The handbrake is the lever usually situated immediately behind the gear lever. Its positions are up for ON and down for OFF. There is a little button on the end of most levers, which should be pressed before applying or releasing this brake lever. (Figure 3.) If it is not pressed when you apply this brake, you will hear a grating noise, which means the teeth are rubbing and the entire mechanism will have to be replaced sooner than would otherwise be necessary.

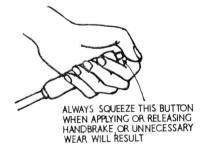

ALWAYS SQUEEZE THIS BUTTON
WHEN APPLYING OR RELEASING
HANDBRAKE, OR UNNECESSARY
WEAR WILL RESULT

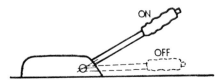

ON

OFF

Figure 3   Typical handbrake, showing 'on' and 'off' positions

Never try to slow or stop the car with this brake when driving normally because it acts only on the rear two wheels and could cause them to lock, thus inducing a skid. Our American friends have a much more descriptive name for this lever. They call it the 'parking brake'.

Direction indicators are usually controlled by a slender stalk mounted on one side or the other of the steering column. The easiest way to decide which way to move this stalk in order to signal your intentions is to remember that, no matter which side of the steering column it may be situated, it should always move in the same direction as that in which you intend to turn the steering wheel.

The horn. This is counted as one of the essential controls because the law states that all vehicles must be fitted with the means of giving an audible warning of approach. Depending on the make or model of your car, the horn button may be located either in the centre of the steering-wheel boss, on the end of the indicator stalk, or perhaps actuated by a second ring situated inside the rim of the steering wheel. (Remember that it is an offence to sound the horn whilst the car is stationary, or between 11.30 pm and 7 am in a built-up area, except to avoid an accident.)

Lights, windscreen wipers, washers, heater etc vary from model to model, even when the same make, as does the facia layout of gauges, speedometer, indicator lamps for ignition, oil and so forth. Often they are labelled or indicated symbolically. If in doubt refer to the handbook for your car. What have here been termed as essential controls are, however, fairly standard.

AUTOMATIC DRIVES

Cars described as 'automatic' fall into two main categories: fully automatic and semi-automatic. And remember that if you pass your driving test on one of these cars your licence will be endorsed for automatic cars only. When driving an automatic, never use the left foot at all. The right foot may be readily transferred from brake to accelerator and vice versa, just as in driving a normal car, but since there is no clutch pedal, the left foot can have a well-deserved rest.

The selector lever, which takes the place of the conventional gear lever, has five positions on most automatics: they are 'Park', 'Reverse', 'Neutral', 'Drive' and 'Lock'. These are self-explanatory, but there is one feature in which automatics may perhaps score over conventional cars, and that is known as the 'kickdown' facility. This operates only when the selector is in 'Drive'. Supposing you wish to overtake a lorry and the road is clear ahead and astern; all you have to do is to kick the accelerator right down to the floor and the automatic gearbox will then change to a lower gear, thus providing the necessary power for overtaking. The box will only change up again when the maximum speed for each gear has been reached, so providing the greatest possible acceleration. Releasing the accelerator at any time will, of course, cause the gearbox to change upwards and speed will then level off.

The British Leyland system used in Minis and 1100s is perhaps even more flexible. Instead of having one 'Lock' position, there are four, and these are equivalent to the conventional gears in an ordinary car. There is therefore the option of holding any particular gear you wish. This box eliminates the unnecessary changes which you would experience with the usual type of automatic car when climbing hills, or on wet or greasy roads.

SMOOTH DRIVING

A car is a relatively complicated piece of mechanism, and it will pay the novice driver handsomely to cultivate as early as he can that indefinable quality which experienced drivers call 'car sympathy'. Examples of this are gentle acceleration (to conserve tyres and suspension), early gentle braking (to save wear on brake lining and tyres), avoidance of jerky driving in general, swerving on corners; in fact, anything which would cause more rapid wear than normal to any part of the car. Try always to drive as if your aged grandmother was on the back seat with a large basket of eggs perched precariously on her lap.

STEERING

Before actually driving the car, there are one or two details you should know about the steering. The impression given by the cinema or television screen when someone is shown driving is that the wheel has to be constantly see-sawing backwards and forwards. This is so blatantly incorrect that whenever you see someone doing this on the screen you may be sure they are not really driving a car at all. A car is so designed that it will automatically follow a straight line (provided the road is straight and level), and one must consciously misalign the wheels in order to turn a corner. It follows, therefore, that if you hold the wheel stationary the car will follow a definite line. It will not wander. Of course, most roads are slightly cambered in order to afford drainage, so the car will tend to follow the camber of the road, ie, it will probably drift slightly to the left (in Britain, where one drives on the left), or to the right on the continent. A slight pressure to meet this tendency is really all that is required, and the correction necessary is so slight as to be hardly noticeable to anyone watching. When you see a learner driver wandering all over the road it is generally because he has not yet come to realise this. It may also perhaps be because he is looking at the kerb and trying to maintain an accurate distance from it. Never do this. The further one looks ahead, the more warning one has of traffic conditions ahead and the longer one has to plan any necessary action in the light of changing traffic conditions. The further you look ahead the straighter will be the course of the car, since you will tend to steer towards where you are looking. It is quite automatic.

Now for turning. Depending upon the make and model of car, there can be up to three and a half revolutions of the steering wheel to turn the front wheels of the car from maximum left to maximum right lock. Therefore, in order to turn a fairly sharp corner it will be necessary to reduce speed first so that you will have sufficient time to really spin that steering wheel around. If you do not get it round fast enough (a common failing with new drivers) you will take the corner much too wide. Practice will make perfect here.

Your instructor will already have told you that the wheel

should be held with the hands positioned at a 'ten-to-two' or 'quarter-to-three' position, and that the wheel should be passed from hand to hand. This may be practised at home between lessons by finding a large plate or round tray about the size of the steering wheel. Hold it as you have been shown how to hold the wheel, then start to turn it first in one direction and then in the other. Make sure nobody is watching, or they will think you require psychoanalysis.

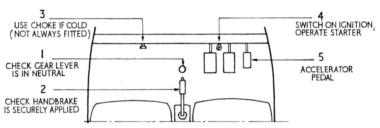

Figure 4   Controls used to start the engine. Numbers show starting sequence for safety

BEFORE STARTING THE ENGINE

If the car has been left with the controls in such a position that the car will move when the starter is actuated, then obviously it will be dangerous to start the engine, for the vehicle could leap forward or backwards and cause injury or damage. Always, therefore, carry out the following checks before touching the starter:

(i) Ensure that the gear lever is set in the neutral position
(ii) Check that the handbrake is fully ON.

Now you may use the ignition key, but *not before carrying out these checks.* Failure to do this would mean failure in the Driving Test.

This book has been so planned that each chapter takes you a little further along the road towards being a good driver. It is not the aim to teach you just to pass the Driving Test, for reasons which will become evident as you read through this book. Passing the Driving Test may be regarded as merely passing out of the kindergarten, and one's driving education really begins *after* it has been successfully negotiated. Do not, please, begin to practise in a car yet, other than with your usual instructor. Unqualified instructors may, in all good faith, do more damage to your confidence, and consequently to your technique, than the saving in the price of lessons would justify.

By all means read right through this book before starting your lessons with a qualified instructor. But do not even try to remember all the detail which you will discover is involved in learning to drive; at least not at this stage. The best method is just to read through the book to get an idea of what is going to be expected of you, first by your instructor and later by the examiner.

Having acquired a rough idea of what good driving is, you can then return to page one and read the first chapter again. Go no further, for this will suffice until after that first driving lesson. After it, you will find it will help a great deal if you read this first chapter through a third time, for as a novice driver at this stage it will seem as if there is an awful lot to remember. This is really the *only* way to do it. And do not be discouraged by the amount of information it seems you have to digest; instead, take courage from the fact that there are obviously many people using the road today with full driving licences who, in an intelligence test, you would leave standing. If they can do it, then so, surely, can you.

Learning to drive entails two separate but interdependent skills, ie, car control, which is a purely manual skill, and roadcraft, which is much more of a mental discipline. Obviously you must master the first before proceeding to the second. In due course you will be able to combine them and it is then that the real skill of driving begins to come into its own.

CHAPTER TWO

Making a Start

In the previous chapter it was stated that the purpose of the clutch was to connect the engine to, or disconnect it from the gearbox. Let us now see how it works.

Figure 5 is an over-simplified sketch of the mechanical functioning of the clutch which, in fact, is a much more complex operation involving the use of multiple springs, special bearings, the application of hydraulics, purpose-designed lining and so on. The aim of this book, however, is not to make you into a first-class mechanic but to set you on the road to becoming a first-class driver, and to achieve this you must from the start learn to drive a car with a certain degree of understanding. This is most easily accomplished by finding out what the various controls actually do, so that you will know, for instance, just what is happening inside the 'works' when you press the clutch pedal either half-way down, or right down to the floor.

In the lower half of the diagram, the clutch pedal is in the 'down' position and it can be seen that the clutch-plate and flywheel are completely separated; there is actually an air gap between them. If the engine were running, it would not drive the car so long as the clutch pedal remained pressed down but would run freely without being under any load.

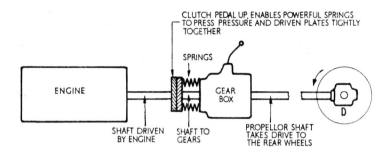

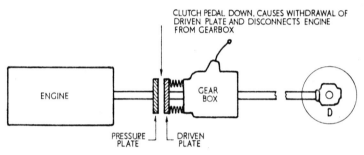

Figure 5 Much simplified diagram showing how the drive is transmitted from the engine by way of the clutch plates, gearbox and propellor shaft to the differential (D) which turns it through 90 degrees in order to drive the rear wheels

Now imagine that the driver has selected first gear. So long as he keeps his foot pressed hard on the clutch pedal the gap between the plates will remain unaltered. Now let him accelerate until the engine is running at, say, 1,000 revolutions a minute (this is a reasonably fast tickover). Bear in mind that the average family saloon weighs the best part of a ton, and imagine what would happen if the driver now snatched his foot off the clutch. The heavy spring behind the clutch-plate would immediately hurl the assembly forward into contact with the flywheel (which is spinning at 1,000 rpm), and it would be a case of the immovable object coming into contact with the irresistible force—perhaps not quite, because the engine can stall and things can break! However, one of several things would be likely to happen:

(i) The sudden application of a load approaching a ton would either stall the engine, or maybe a vital part of it would fracture.

(ii) Damage could result to the clutch itself (lining ruined etc).

(iii) The shaft on which the clutch is mounted could fracture.

(iv) Something inside the gearbox could be broken.

(v) The propeller shaft, or its couplings, could fracture.

Other equally horrifying things could conceivably happen, and even if nothing actually broke, the least that could occur (if you were lucky) is that the car would suddenly leap forward. Because first gear is engaged (which possesses the greatest power), acceleration would be vivid, dislodging the driver's foot from the accelerator pedal. Instinctively he would try to steady it, but as this is extremely difficult in a jerking car progress would probably be made in a series of convulsive jumps reminiscent of early silent comedy films. *So we make a note never to jump off the clutch.*

Now consider what happens when the driver *gently* releases the clutch pedal. As his foot comes slowly off the pedal, the spring begins to take the clutch-plate forward on its shaft until it is about to touch the already spinning flywheel. At this point (known as the 'point of contact') there is some slip between the two surfaces of the flywheel and the clutch-plate. Because the clutch lining behaves in the same manner as brake linings, there will also be some slight grip. Hence, although the flywheel is actually slipping over the surface of the clutch-plate, it will still be trying to make the clutch-plate turn with it. Now if the driver lifts his foot even more gently off the pedal, thus permitting the powerful spring behind the clutch to press forward with a steadily increasing force, the result will be that the load (the weight of the car) is gradually applied to the engine via the flywheel and the shaft upon which it is mounted. (See upper half of Figure 5.) Provided nothing is now preventing the car from actually moving, such as the handbrake being in the ON position, the car will begin to move gently forward at a speed proportional to the engine revs and the degree of clutch-pedal lift. If the revs are maintained at a constant figure (suppose the 1,000 rpm is unaltered), then the car can be made to either edge forward very slowly by letting the clutch up only just beyond the point of contact, or to move at the speed determined by the engine speed when the clutch is in the 'fully engaged' position, ie, the clutch pedal in its normal 'up' position.

There are still some further points to be borne in mind even though the working of the clutch has now been grasped. For instance, when the pedal is at the 'point of contact' and there is slip between the spinning surface of the flywheel and the clutch lining, there is a degree of friction present and, where there is friction, heat is also being generated. Friction and heat mean wear, and the longer you keep the unfortunate clutch in this position, the greater will be the heat generated and the heavier will be the wear on the surfaces which are sliding against each other. We deduce, therefore, that the 'point of contact' is not a good position in which to hold the clutch pedal for any length of time. The lining would very soon give up the ghost, and this would mean a relatively expensive repair. Clutch linings themselves are not all that expensive, but renewal of them induces a major dismantling job; on many cars it even means removal of the engine to get at the 'works' which have to be replaced. The kind of bill you could expect might even read: 'Clutch plate £1·50; labour £30·00, and with such bills in prospect one rapidly learns to use the clutch with a high degree of circumspection.

Unfortunately it is necessary when garaging a car or parking in a crowded car park, or in similarly ticklish situations, to make use of a technique known as 'clutch control'. This was described a couple of paragraphs ago and is most easily summarised as follows: keep the engine revs quite steady at about 1,000 or a little over and control the speed of the car by varying the height of the clutch pedal delicately between the 'point of contact' position and the 'fully up' position. In a later chapter some suggestions will be offered for exercises in this technique.

We have now seen how the car can be made to move. In Chapter 1 it was stated that a gearbox was necessary in order to take maximum advantage of the power range of the engine. Now although it was necessary to know basically how a clutch worked, because you have to make use of its variable characteristics, it is by no means essential to understand just what actually goes on inside the gearbox. All that is required from you as a driver is to know:

(i) the position of the gear lever for any particular gear on your car, and (ii) when to change gear (upwards or downwards).

The gear lever positions shown in Figure 2 on page 13 are applicable to almost all conventional cars, including those which have the gear lever mounted on the steering column instead of on the floor of the car. These have become unpopular in recent years, though, and at least whilst learning you will be unlikely to encounter such a layout.

Engine speeds can vary from below 1,000 rpm to over 6,000 rpm, but there is a limited range of revolutions over which any engine will develop its peak pulling power. Because of this limitation, if the engine were connected directly to the wheels which drive the car along the road we would have only one range of speed and one range of power dependent upon this speed. For this reason there must be interposed between the engine and the wheels a device which will enable us to make optimum use of the engine's power no matter what the circumstances of driving may be, whether it is just to maintain speed along a level road, which uses little power; to climb a steep hill, which requires a lot of power; or to accelerate away from rest, necessitating plenty of power, to, say, 6o mph, and then merely maintain that speed in 'top' gear, which uses least power. Cars may, as we have seen already, have from three to five gears, and lorries capable of carrying heavy loads will have even more, maybe as many as ten. All that the reverse gear does is to reverse the direction of rotation of the propeller shaft, so that the car goes backwards. Since one never normally wishes to go hurtling backwards, this is usually a very low gear. Often manufacturers save money by making this gear the same ratio as first gear, which of course means that it will have the same power and speed range. A neutral position, in which no gear is selected by the lever, is always provided. This enables one to run the engine of the car without holding down the clutch in order to disconnect the engine from the gearbox. Neutral is therefore, in fact, 'No Gear Engaged'; it is just easier and quicker to say, and maybe sounds more technical.

EMERGENCY DRILL

Paradoxically, the first thing to learn before actually starting to move the car at all is how to stop it in an emergency. When one is driving along, things can happen with disconcerting suddenness; this is all very well so long as a qualified instructor is sitting beside you in a dual-controlled car, but if the car is not fitted with 'duals', or the person beside you is not a qualified instructor trained to react correctly in any given set of circumstances, then almost any unforeseen situation could be a potentially dangerous one. The essential movement you must learn before even attempting to move off is to transfer your right foot quickly from the accelerator pedal to the brake pedal. One never uses the left foot on the brake pedal for reasons which will become obvious as more skill is acquired. Besides, so long as one remains sane, one should not need to accelerate and brake at the same time (in normal driving!). Hence the right foot looks after the accelerator and brakes, whilst the left is reserved for the clutch pedal. You will soon find that the left foot will have quite enough to do without bothering about slowing or stopping the car.

In any emergency which may occur at the low speeds you will be using to start with, it does not really matter from a safety point of view if you forget to depress the clutch pedal when stopping the car. From a mechanical point of view, however, it is highly desirable because, should you forget, you will stop the car with the engine still connected to the gearbox (which in turn is connected to the wheels which drive the car along the road). It follows, therefore, that if you stop the wheels turning with the clutch pedal in the UP, or 'engaged' position, you will stall the engine—and stalling never does an engine the slightest bit of good. Hence we can try to remember, 'When in doubt, both feet out'. Practise this several times without the engine running before trying to drive the car. Your instructor will be delighted at your safety consciousness and, even better, you will have already carried out the drill for the dreaded 'Emergency Stop' which occurs during the Driving Test. Incidentally, do not expect your instructor to let you practise emergency stops from speeds around 30 and 40 mph as a regular part of your lessons once you are competent to drive at such speeds, because emergency stops are a considerable strain on various vitals of the car, as well as on the tyres and brakes. They are also rather unnerving to unsuspecting pedestrians or people in the vicinity, who are apt to wonder where the accident is about to happen when they hear tyres and brakes protesting shrilly.

A good instructor will leave such practice until only a

lesson or two before your actual driving test, and will even then select carefully where emergency stops are to be carried out, ie, on quiet roads away from a densely populated area, and with no traffic at all behind the car.

Now that you feel you know exactly what to do in order to stop the car, we can consider the correct procedure for moving off.

PRECAUTIONS BEFORE MOVING OFF

It is absolutely essential for you consciously to school yourself into being one hundred per cent safety minded from the very beginning of your driving career. If you do so you will rapidly find yourself acquiring good driving habits as a matter of course. Habits are difficult things to abolish, so the sooner you pick up good ones related to driving the better the progress you will make as a driver. Further, not only will you become a good driver, but you will be much more likely to remain one.

Before we start the car off from the kerb for the first time, then, let us assume that the engine is already running. We saw how to start it at the end of the last chapter. The mirror should, of course, already be adjusted as was recommended in Chapter 1.

If the engine is running, you will have to disengage the clutch (put the left-hand pedal right down to the floor—remember?) This enables first gear to be selected. Now do nothing further until you have carried out the following safety checks:

(i) Look in the rear-view mirror to ensure that no traffic is likely to be endangered when you move out from the kerb

(ii) Glance over the right shoulder in order to check that nothing (such as a cycle, a child on a scooter, or anything similar) is actually about to pass your car from the rear.

Having assured yourself that it is in fact safe to leave the kerb, you now release the handbrake completely (don't

27

forget the little button on its end), and begin to let the clutch pedal up gently until the point of contact is reached. Now let it up even more gently, and you will find that the car begins to move forward slowly. In order that smoothness of progress may be maintained at this stage it will have been necessary to squeeze the accelerator gently as you lifted the clutch, but do not overdo it at this stage. Practice at moving off a few times will soon give you the 'feel' of these two controls: the clutch and the accelerator. A useful hint to remember in connection with these is that, as a general rule, when the clutch is depressed the accelerator must be released, and vice versa. This is so that the engine note will stay reasonably steady, or to put it another way, in order that engine revs will not rise unduly when the clutch is disengaged (thus disconnecting the engine effectively from the wheels of the car).

BRAKING AT SLOW SPEED

The car is now moving slowly along the road in first gear. Try to vary its speed smoothly with the accelerator. You will find this fairly difficult to achieve at first, since the powerful first gear offers lively acceleration. Just a touch on the accelerator pedal and the car will surge forward. Do not let this alarm you. To take a breathing spell and get used to the idea of what we have just done, let us now pretend to pull in to the side of the road. Before even touching the brake pedal it is necessary to check in the rear-view mirror to make sure that when we slow or stop the car we will not be presenting a hazard to any traffic which may be behind us. ALWAYS do this; it is one of the good driving habits referred to earlier, and its omission would automatically mean failure in the Driving Test. It is also very foolish to brake without first checking the mirror, since an accident could result.

Now, having checked that all is safe behind, transfer the

right foot from the accelerator pedal to the brake pedal and squeeze gently. Braking is progressive, which means that the harder you press the brake pedal, the more rapidly will the car slow down and stop. If you maintain the pressure, you will notice that the car will come to rest with a jerk. We have already agreed that jerky driving of any kind is undesirable, so this is a small point which must be attended to with consistent regularity until you have not only acquired proficiency at it, but do it automatically. Smooth stopping of the vehicle is achieved by guessing at the actual point at which the car will finally stop, then releasing the pressure on the brake pedal just as that point is being reached. This may sound a bit of a hit-and-miss sort of operation, but rest assured that although you may find it slightly difficult at first, and may sometimes even forget to do it, you will get better and better at it until you do not even notice yourself doing it. Furthermore, you will achieve an accuracy that you did not believe possible when you started to do it.

Now, before you try doing all this in the car with your instructor, read all this through again. When you have practised it in the car with him, read it over once or twice more in order to recapitulate what you have been doing whilst actually driving the vehicle. By revising like this, your understanding of the functions of the controls and the reasons for carrying out certain actions in the sequence described will become much clearer.

There are pupils who listen to their instructor sitting beside them in the car without really understanding just what the poor chap is trying his hardest to put over to them. But they let him go on talking in the fond hope that if he does it long enough something will jell in their minds. Do not under any circumstances do this. If you have not understood what he was trying to explain, then first refer to the appropriate section of this book and read it slowly through in your own time, thinking hard about what you are reading.

On the other hand, if there is something in the book with which you have difficulty, then do not hesitate to show the relevant passage to your instructor during your next lesson and ask him to explain it. If it is merely the reason behind a certain sequence of actions, then remember there is always at least one very good purpose behind them—sometimes as many as half-a-dozen. He will be delighted to give you chapter and verse, where necessary.

Before your next lesson you should read those sections in the Highway Code which deal with Moving Off, Driving Along, Use of the Mirror, and Stopping. Also refer to the paragraphs which define where one must not park or cause the car to wait. As you read each paragraph, try to do so slowly, and try to discover the reason behind any Dos or Don'ts which you come across. You will find that in this way you will remember the advice contained in it much more easily than if you just tried to learn it as a lesson to be repeated to the examiner during your driving test.

PRACTICE

At this stage you will have read through the Highway Code more than once, and will begin to get the idea behind the uses of all the controls, although your competence in their actual use will be somewhat sketchy. Don't worry. Practice is what you need now.

This is the stage at which you can, with advantage, try to start and stop the car repeatedly. You can do this between lessons with your instructor if you have a relative who is willing to permit you to risk his precious vehicle. To conform with the law, a qualified driver must always be sitting beside you when you undertake any practice at all of this kind. Also, that qualified driver should be able to reach the handbrake and ignition key.

Do not attempt to perform any manoeuvre other than

starting the engine, checking for safety and moving off from the kerb. Once the car is moving, try not to panic regarding the absence of your trusted instructor, but look in your mirror to check for safety before stopping, then apply the brakes (right foot off accelerator and on to footbrake), left foot down to disengage the clutch, and bring the car to a smooth halt at the side of the road.

Provided you pause and think before actually moving the car, and do not panic when you find it actually moving, all should be well. Don't rush anything. Nobody is hustling you, and the owner of the car would prefer you to take your time and do the thing carefully and correctly rather than rush and fumble uncertainly with the possibility of kangaroo starts and jerky stops. He will also be peeved if you strike the kerb. Tyres are expensive.

Take your time, and repeat this starting and stopping until both you and your companion are satisfied that you are actually making progress. There is no need to run before you can walk, and starting and stopping the car are the 'walking' which is so vital at this juncture. It also means that you will have plenty of confidence for your next lesson.

CHAPTER THREE

Elementary Driving

As a result of the previous chapter (and a lot of practice!) you are now able to start the car, move off from the kerb, drive along in first gear, and stop at a place where it was safe to do so. You are also able to halt the car should any emergency arise.

The next thing to appreciate is that you should at all times be as fully aware of what traffic is behind you as of what is in front. In fact, unless you are always aware of the complete traffiic picture all around you on the road, and can assess the situation continually whilst driving along, then your driving is not yet safe enough to enable you to drive unaccompanied.

The rear-view mirror, for instance, should be checked quickly every few seconds, and the necessity for this is shown by the following example. Imagine you are driving along a motorway in a saloon car at a speed of 60 mph. Approximately a mile ahead is a lorry in the slow (left-hand) lane, doing 30 mph. You correctly glance in your mirror to see a vehicle some distance behind you; it looks quite small because it is so far away (maybe half a mile), so you decide to pull out into the middle lane (there are usually three lanes available) in order to overtake the lorry. The speed difference between your vehicle and the lorry is 30 mph, so it will take you a full two minutes to draw level with the lorry. While you are still catching up with it you are suddenly startled to see something flash past on your right and disappear into the distance ahead. It was the vehicle you had seen in your mirror and which had appeared so very innocuous. Actually it was a high-performance sportscar, many of which are today capable of over 150 mph, and the driver was disregarding the motorway rules which include the blanket speed limit of 70 mph. You would have been fortunate in this instance in having three lanes available, otherwise the consequence of your misjudgement of the sportscar's speed could have been disastrous. His speed excess over yours was perhaps as much as a hundred miles an hour—and you had thought you were moving rather fast!

Hence, then, the reason for watching that mirror like a hawk, and intelligently assessing the information with which it is able to supply you continuously. Admittedly, the instance just given may appear to be exaggerated, but remember that such cases can and do occur. The Highway Code tells you the occasions when it is obligatory to use your mirror, and these may be summarised, briefly, as EVERY occasion upon which you intend to alter the course or speed of your vehicle. The main point to note is that the mirror should be used early enough to enable you to make a change of plan if necessary BEFORE you even signal your intention to carry out whatever manoeuvre you had in mind. That, of course, is in addition to using it every few seconds in normal driving along. The importance of frequent reference to the rear-view mirror cannot be over-emphasised and as you become more skilled with the controls and learn to handle the car in traffic, you will begin to realise just how vital that mirror really is. It is the car driver's best friend.

SMOOTH USE OF CONTROLS

The reasons why it is necessary to cultivate a smooth style of driving were explained in Chapter 1 and the manner in which this can be done was briefly referred to in Chapter 2. The whole secret of it lies in the gentle and intelligent use of the three pedals.

Figure 6   Smooth use of the accelerator calls for the heel of the right foot to rest on the car floor, with the ball of the foot on the pedal

    (i) Never accelerate harshly
    (ii) Never brake harshly
    (iii) Cultivate the habit of using the clutch gently.

Read again, in Chapter 2, the passage about the necessity for releasing the accelerator when depressing the clutch and try to imagine that you are using your feet like a duck, ie, as the left foot comes up the right one must go down, and vice versa. Keep your heels pivoted on the floor of the car and practise the movements in a stationary car until they become instinctive. (See Figure 6.)

Gear changes are carried out by 'de-clutching', changing gear, and then re-engaging the clutch when the new gear is selected, so that every time you change gear you will have to put the left foot down to the floor whilst you release the accelerator by lifting the right foot; then when the gear change has been made, let the clutch gently back whilst at the same time accelerating gently but firmly.

GEAR CHANGES—UPWARDS

The basic principle of gear changing has just been explained, but now let us consider in detail how it is carried out in actual driving. There are two main methods of driving on an ordinary highway (as opposed to competition driving), and these are known as Economy Driving and Performance Driving. The first is self-explanatory; one naturally wishes to drive as a general rule in the most economical manner consistent with safety, but a novice driver may well be forgiven for feeling that this is hardly the time or place to introduce Performance Driving. Think about it for a moment, though. How often have you been in a car driven by someone else and sat at a road junction behind a car wearing L plates? It has taken the poor learner driver some time to get his car moving; meanwhile the traffic behind him has become increasingly impatient and the driver of the car in which you were sitting has no doubt been making uncomplimentary remarks about L drivers and their instructors in general. No one would consciously wish to be the cause of a traffic jam, and this is where Performance Driving comes into the picture. Here is a brief description of each method:

Economy Driving necessitates changing gear upwards as soon as may be practical without causing the engine to labour in any particular gear. In other words, we just get the car moving comfortably in first gear, change at once to second, pick up a little more speed (dependent upon the model and type of gearbox), change to third gear, pick up more speed, then up to fourth and so on. The general idea is to reach top gear in as little time and distance as possible, consistent with not overloading the engine.

Performance Driving, on the other hand, implies hard acceleration in order that as much speed as possible may be achieved in each of the gears. In this method of driving we move off in first gear, then accelerate hard and hold first gear until perhaps 15 or 20 mph has been reached, then a quick change to second followed immediately by brisk acceleration up over maybe 30 mph and so on. When you try both methods you will realise just why the first one is called the Economy method, and you will be surprised at how a quite ordinary family saloon can be made to get away from a junction the moment it is safe to do so, and how quickly it can pick up the speed of the traffic already using the main road which it has just joined.

Having explained all this, let us decide to use only the Economy method for the present until your instructor decides that you are ready to experiment with somewhat more brisk methods of dealing with these gear changes.

Without going into quite complicated technical details concerning the gearbox, it may be helpful to remember that a gear change is always effected by disconnecting one gear train and connecting another. In a conventional gearbox this means that a moving part has to be brought into contact with a stationary part. The manufacturers in their wisdom have compensated for this apparently potentially disastrous state of affairs by introducing a component known as the 'synchromesh'. Its job in life is to try to equalise the speed of the two parts which are to be brought into contact, and to do this it very obviously requires time. For this reason, one never snatches the gear lever from one position to another. The movement of the gear lever should always be smooth, and, ideally, with a momentary pause in neutral as progression is made from one gear to another. This applies equally to upward or downward changes. Before we actually deal with a gear change on the move, there is one habit the novice driver should be warned about. Many drivers subconsciously acquire the bad and lazy habit of resting a hand on the gear lever while they are driving along, and there are two very good reasons why you should never allow yourself to get into such a habit. First, your hands should be on the wheel at all times except when actually removing one of them to deal with a control or a switch. Second, whilst your hand is resting on the gear lever a component called the selector fork is being forced into contact with moving parts. This should not be allowed to happen, as it will result in unnecessary wear on the selector forks, which can cause the gears to become disengaged. This is commonly known as 'jumping out of gear', and can be a very expensive fault to cure, since it entails dismantling the gearbox—a job to be entrusted to only a skilled mechanic. In many cars it even means that the whole engine and gearbox assembly has to be completely removed from the car.

You should now be able to start and stop the car, drive it along in a reasonably straight line, using the mirror intelligently, and change gear at appropriate times and speeds. The next step is to acquire a sound knowledge of procedure at turns, both left and right. There are a variety of different types of turns and each one must be negotiated in an individual manner, although the basic principle remains the same throughout. There are gentle turns, sharp ones, uphill and downhill turns, turns into or out of major roads at T junctions, crossroads, traffic lights, and so on. Here is the general basic drill for all of them:

        (i) Mirror
        (ii) Signal
        (iii) Manoeuvre

Remember that no matter what kind of a turn you are contemplating, you will in all probability have to slow down, however slightly, in order to complete it competently, so remember also the advice in earlier chapters and *use that mirror* before taking your foot off the accelerator or signalling your intention. Having signalled, you can then start the business of changing gear downwards, slowing, changing lane if necessary, and so forth, but mirror always takes priority over everything (except steering to avoid a collision).

THE LEFT TURN

Your instructor will at first certainly arrange matters so that nearly all the turns you negotiate are gentle ones. Then, as he finds you are dealing with these in an increasingly competent manner, he will take you to places where he knows there are more difficult and sharper ones. The secret of taking a car round corners neatly is merely that the sharper a corner is, the more slowly it should be taken. There are one or two obvious points which will emerge as you acquire more experience, one of them being that in left turns it is deceptively easy to misplace the car, resulting in either the rear wheels riding over the kerb or the car swinging too wide on the corner and consequently presenting a hazard to oncoming traffic.

Since there is an appreciable distance between the front and rear wheels of any car, and because the front wheels are steerable and the rear ones are not, it becomes obvious, when you think about it, that the two pairs of wheels will be unable to follow exactly in the same set of tracks in a corner. To compensate for this, it is necessary that the car be correctly placed if the corner is to be neatly negotiated. The ideal for a left-hand corner is roughly two or three feet out from the left-hand kerb, the actual distance depending upon the type of car you are driving. Obviously, one would position a Mini much closer to the kerb than, say, a large American car. If the latter were placed in the same position as a Mini for the same corner, the rear wheels would undoubtedly endanger the toes of unfortunate pedestrians, and the driver would be likely to damage the walls of his tyres. The longer a vehicle, the further from the kerb it must be positioned before making a turn. This is the reason why articulated lorries should be given a wide berth in such circumstances; they often require the whole road for quite a simple turn—at least it would be simple to you in a much smaller vehicle.

The fault of swinging too wide on a left-hand corner is commonly caused by attempting to take the corner too fast, so the remedy for that is even simpler.

RIGHT-HAND TURNS

Whereas one takes a left-hand corner fairly close to the kerb so that the car will be on its 'own side' of the road when it emerges from the corner, the problem is slightly more complicated when turning right. Obviously, one still wishes to emerge from the corner on the correct side of the road, so for this reason the corner must be taken fairly wide; in other words, the actual turn is not quite so tight as the left-hand one. The matter of placing the car or 'setting it up' for the corner is where most people find difficulty.

Assuming that the car is proceeding northwards, here is what happens. Driver decides to take the next right turn, so first uses his rear-view mirror before signalling his intention to turn right. When satisfied that no other vehicle is about to overtake him, he signals for his right turn, ensuring that he is giving the drivers of other vehicles in the vicinity plenty of time to observe his signal and plan their own actions accordingly. (Incidentally, this is one of the few occasions when another vehicle can legally overtake him on his left.) Having signalled, he starts to reduce speed and, after checking his mirror again, he can change into the right-hand lane (if he sees that it is safe to do so). Early observation will have told him just how sharp a corner he has decided to negotiate, and he will now change down into the appropriate gear for the corner. Before starting the turn he must use the mirror again, and look well ahead to check for oncoming traffic. Should there be any oncoming traffic, he must wait for it to pass by before commencing his turn (remember para 78 of the Code says 'wait until there is a safe gap between you and any oncoming vehicle'). If he has to wait, he should remember not to fall into the trap of letting the car roll forward too far, or the corner will become a very difficult one for him; the ideal spot at which to wait for other traffic to clear is just before the centre-line of the road into which he intends to turn. Now when all is clear, the driver may start his car moving again. Of course if he has had to stop moving, he will move off again in first gear, using gentle acceleration all the way round the corner and not changing gear until his wheels are straightening up again.

All this sounds quite a lot for a novice to remember, but is very easily summarised.

(i) Use the mirror often—and always before you signal or change course

(ii) Slow and get into the correct lane early

(iii) Make sure you are in the correct gear well before the corner

(iv) Wait for oncoming traffic to pass

(v) When taking the turn, take it fairly wide, and complete the turn on your own side of the road.

CHANGING GEAR DOWNWARDS

You will have noticed already that when driving along in a low gear the revs are relatively high compared with when the car is in one of the higher gears. If one goes too fast in first gear, for instance the engine positively screams in protest.

Now imagine we are approaching a corner that has to be taken at a lower speed than that at which we are moving at the moment. Obviously we will need a lower gear, so that after negotiating the corner we will be in a gear which has ample acceleration to enable the car to pick up speed again the moment it is called upon to do so. A lower gear implies, usually, a lower speed, but we do not reduce the speed of the car merely by changing to a lower gear; that is what the brakes are for. This has already been explained. Hence we reduce the speed of the vehicle by using the brakes as necessary. When the appropriate speed for the next lowest gear has been achieved, declutch, select the appropriate gear, and accelerate slightly as you raise the clutch pedal. A certain amount of practice will be needed to get the knack of knowing just how much to accelerate as you release the clutch gently. The reason for accelerating in this case is so that the engine will be running at the necessary speed to match the road speed of the car for the gear you have just selected.

The only time one normally uses the gears to slow the car in normal driving, as opposed to competition driving, is in an emergency—if, for instance, the brakes should become wholly or partly ineffective. Remember, though, that if they do, it is very probably your own fault. Such things are generally due to lack of proper maintenance. If your car is regularly and properly serviced, your brakes should not fail, and so no such emergency should ever arise. The only reason that mention has been made of slowing the car by means of the gears is so that you should be aware that this is a method which may be adapted *in an emergency*. On a very long and steep hill (Porlock, parts of Devon, Cornwall, the Lake District, Yorkshire, Scotland; there are plenty that you will meet later on!) brakes can fade; this is a phenomenon in which excessive heat causes the brake linings to acquire a glaze and so reduces their efficiency. It can be very alarming if you are not aware of what is happening, and it is then not the slightest use pressing the brake pedal harder in the fond hope that this will result in a decrease of speed. It may even result in the very opposite. Resolve, then, that if you see a sign indicating a steep hill ahead and advising the use of a low gear, to change into that gear early so that you will already be using a suitable gear when starting to descend the steep slope.

CHAPTER FOUR

Low-speed Manœuvres

The drill you have carried out so far in moving the car away from the kerb is the most elementary type possible, because every time you have done so the car has been on a reasonably level surface in order to make things easy for you. Now let us take things a step further. Suppose the car is stationary facing uphill. Obviously the moment the handbrake is released, it will roll backwards, with perhaps disastrous results.

If we refer back to the description of how a clutch works, it will be noted that when the pedal is lifted to the 'point of contact', the clutch is just taking the weight of the car, and this is the point at which the handbrake can safely be released. The precise position of the pedal for the point of contact is easy to establish, for at this point there will be some slight braking effect upon the engine, with a resulting drop in the note which it emits. It is easier still on cars with Hydrolastic suspension, such as the 1100s, 1800s, Maxis and so on of British Leyland, for owing to their suspension peculiarities, the nose of the car will begin to rise when the clutch is at the point of contact. This is all very well when you are first becoming accustomed to the drill, but you should try to train yourself to listen to the engine note as well. You will then be able to perform successful hill starts regardless of what type of car you happen to be driving. As with everything else associated with driving, it is only practice which will help you to become proficient at this.

Now supposing the car has been facing downhill. When the handbrake was removed it would immediately have run forwards out of control. The car is only regarded as completely under control, remember, when it does what *you* cause it to do—not when it does something involuntarily. This type of start is even easier than the previous one.

For a downhill start it is only necessary to hold the car on the footbrake while the handbrake is released, then, after checking for safety, to move the right foot from the footbrake pedal to the accelerator whilst letting the clutch pedal back smoothly. The essential thing to remember, no matter how skilfully you are able to perform both these evolutions, is to check your rear-view mirror and look over your shoulder before permitting the car to move at all.

Sometimes it is necessary for a turn to be made into another road which slopes upwards or downwards from the road out of which one is turning. In this case the speed of the vehicle must be reduced perhaps a great deal more than if the turn was on a level surface, and use is made of clutch control. (Please refer back to this section.) Ask your instructor to select a few such corners for you to use as practice and try to remember just what you did when moving off from a stationary position. You may find it a little difficult at first, but here again practice will quickly pay off. If you fail to practise these turns, you will acquire the habit of taking corners without complete car control; this results in an incorrect speed for the corner and probably taking it too wide, with the risk of not only failure in the Driving Test, but the possibility of accident at some future date.

REVERSING

The time will come when your instructor will explain about reversing. Most instructors have their own methods of teaching this, so to avoid any possibility of conflict with them only the essential points will be touched on here to assist you and to amplify what your instructor will tell you.

When reversing, never try to drive the car backwards at too high a speed. Remember that clutch control technique again and it will pay handsome dividends.

Strange thought it may seem, many people are confused between their left and right hands—particularly when the car is going backwards. Normally all that one has to bear in mind is that, in Britain, one still drives on the left-hand side of the road. If the car is going slowly enough (as it should be if your clutch control is effective) you will have ample time to remember this basic fact and act accordingly. Many people also have some trouble in deciding which way to turn the steering wheel so that the car will go in the direction they wish. Again there is a simple tip which will help you if you are having this kind of trouble. Sit well over to the right-hand side of the driver's seat in an attitude which enables you to look through the centre of the rear window and place the right hand at twelve o'clock on the steering wheel. Now all you have to do is to move that hand in the direction which you want the rear end of the car to follow. Sit and think about this for a moment or two before you actually begin to reverse, and the chances of your making a mistake are then very slim indeed.

At first, your instructor will ask you to reverse in a straight line, since this is the easiest type of reverse. Before doing so there is one point to note. When going backwards, the steering is being done by the 'trailing' wheels rather than the 'leading' ones, therefore the 'trailing' end of the car will alter course much more rapidly than the 'leading' end. Furthermore, only slight corrections of the steering wheel will be necessary to maintain a straight course. The slightest over-correction will result in rather prompt response on the part of the car, so that unless you are going very slowly indeed the rear of the vehicle will either mount the kerb or swing out into the road. Hence the need for even more careful clutch control. According to the Road Traffic Act, there is no restriction on the distance a vehicle is permitted to reverse provided it does not constitute a danger to other traffic, so since your instructor will have selected a safe area in which you can practise your early efforts at reversing, you need have little or no worries on that score. One habit you should acquire at the outset, however, is to check ahead frequently to ensure that you are not likely to impede oncoming traffic (remember that when you move your steering wheel to the right the rear of the car will swing to the right, ie, out into the road and hence into the probable path of other traffic).

REVERSING TO THE LEFT

There are normally three ways of turning the car round to face in the opposite direction, and one of them is to drive past a side road on the left, reverse into it, and then drive out again turning to the right as you do so, thus enabling you to go back the way you have just come. This is one of the exercises you will be asked to carry out during your driving test in order to demonstrate your ability to drive the car backwards in safety and with a fair degree of accuracy. Since you have already practised reversing in a straight line, you will be familiar with the techniques required to move the car safely back at a fairly low speed. All that now remains is to carry out this manoeuvre, and at the same time steer the car to the left so as to negotiate the corner safely. To do so, it is first necessary to check for safety *before* beginning the turn, because when applying left lock to the steering wheel the bonnet of the car is going to swing out to the right into the road and possibly into the path of oncoming traffic. Think about this for a moment. Do not just accept any statement about the behaviour of a car without due consideration, for then you will know next time just what will happen. Now, having checked for safety, started to move the car and approaching the corner, one therefore rechecks again for safety by looking forward. If satisfied, you can begin the actual turn. The correct moment to do this is usually when the nearside kerb is just disappearing as you look over your left shoulder, but your instructor will give you more precise guidance according to the type of car you are driving.

Where most people find a certain amount of difficulty is not in actually deciding when to start the turn, but in when to straighten up the wheels so that the car will continue its course parallel to the kerb after entering the new road. The only way to overcome this difficulty is by regular and method-ical practice. It will help a great deal if you can find a patch of deserted ground for these low-speed practice sessions, and a few large grocery cartons will be found useful if you space them out as markers.

Reference to Figure 7 will make it obvious why one should continue to reverse for some distance, say about 30ft or so into the new road. If you stopped the car only just after negotiating the corner, the following would be the result:

(a) contravention of Para 97 (2) of the Highway Code, which clearly states that you should not park or let your vehicle stand at or near a junction.

(b) it would be incorrectly placed for negotiation of the ensuing right turn into the major road.

(c) it would undoubtedly impair the vision of pedestrians, and maybe even endanger them at the junction.

For these reasons you should drive it back parallel to the kerb until at least two to three car-lengths past the corner. Accuracy on the corner as required by the examiner is merely 'reasonable', which may safely be taken as two to three feet out from the kerb whilst turning. The car should come to rest in approximately a parking position relative to the kerb.

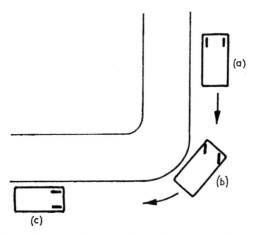

Figure 7 Reversing practice: at the point of starting the turn (b) look both ahead and astern to make sure you will not swing the front of the car into the path of passing traffic, then check that the nearside rear wheel will not strike the kerb and perhaps damage the tyre. On completion of the reverse (c), see that the car is parked at a suitable distance from the corner

REVERSING TO THE RIGHT

When driving a private car of conventional design, one does not normally hesitate to reverse into a side road on the left as, rear visibility being good (unlike ancient vehicles which had pokey little rear windows), the fact that one is reversing against the traffic stream is of little consequence. It is easy to check for safety and stop if necessary. With a van, which has more restricted visibility, or a loaded shooting brake, or any other vehicle which may impair the driver's vision to the rear, the normal procedure is to reverse into a side road on the right. In order to do so safely, after checking the rear-view mirror and signalling that a right turn is intended, the vehicle is pulled in at the right-hand side of the road a little beyond the road into which it is intended to reverse. Please note that when the vehicle is now reversed, it will be travelling *with* the traffic stream, and not against it. In this instance the driver is permitted to open his door and look out, so that he can watch the distance of his wheels from the kerb.

The actual turn is, of course, just like the left-hand reverse except that the steering wheel has to be turned in the opposite direction. If this seems like a blinding glimpse of the obvious, don't laugh until you have tried it, and if you do get it correct the very first time you will then be entitled to smile. After having practised the left-hand reverse many times, most people make an awful mess of the right-hand reverse when they first try it. Even if they turn the wheel the correct way, they are often lulled into a false sense of security because they find they can actually watch the kerb. They therefore tend to let the car get much too close to it, with the result that they either have to go forward to their original position and try again, or risk damaging their tyres. If you ever do find yourself too close to a kerb, do not hesitate to go forward and try again. It is a very much safer action than scraping the tyres against the kerb and causing damage to the walls of the tyres. Nothing might happen for some time —until the car was driven fast; then a burst could result, with the possibility of fatal results. Always regard it as a demonstration of rank bad driving to let your tyres touch the kerb, and you will not only save yourself money, but also avoid endangering your own life or that of others.

As in the left-hand reverse, the vehicle should proceed backwards parallel to the kerb until two to three lengths back from the corner. This is for exactly the same reasons that the car was placed well back in the left-hand turn.

Now comes what is perhaps the only potentially dangerous portion of this manoeuvre. It is necessary, in order to turn left into the major road, to pull out from the *wrong side* of the road on which you are at present parked, cross this road, and place the vehicle for a left-hand turn. If the driver is on his own, he must use the left-hand wing mirror, with which such vehicles are compulsorily fitted, as well as looking back through the rear window. If loaded he may have to crane over towards the passenger's side of the vehicle in order to ensure that all is safe before he moves. If he has a passenger, he can ask the passenger to warn him of the approach of other traffic from the rear. Once assured that it is safe to move the vehicle, position can be taken up for the left-hand turn, and procedure from then onwards reverts to normal.

TURNING THE CAR IN THE ROAD

The second method of turning the car to face in the opposite direction is to use the forward and reverse gears and the steering wheel. This can be practised at any time after clutch control has been mastered, and your instructor will normally select a little-used and fairly wide road for your initial attempts. The main point to bear in mind in this, and in fact with any low-speed manoeuvres, is not to be afraid to really spin that steering wheel. Half-hearted attempts will result in extremely poor turns which will fail to get the car round as much as required. The trick is to use clutch control very carefully so that the car moves very slowly indeed and so gives you time in which to get the steering wheel right round on to full lock. Knowing this, the actual manoeuvre should be child's play. Whatever you are about to do, of course, the very first point is to check for safety before attempting to move the car. Look up and down the road, and if any other traffic is coming, don't move. Later, when you have started the turn in the road, if any traffic appears on your side of the road, get over to the other side and wait until it is clear before continuing. If the traffic which has appeared is on the other side of the road, then remain where you are until it has passed. Of course this advice will be dependent upon how far away you can see the other traffic. If in doubt, don't move.

After having checked for safety, start the car moving gently forward under superb clutch control, and before it has gone forward more than two or three feet, you should have the steering wheel round on full right lock, thus giving the car the remainder of the width of the road in which to turn. As the far kerb approaches, ie, when there is only a couple of feet or so to go, quickly spin the wheel back to the left as far as it will go, but on no account let the car take charge. By this is meant that you should still maintain that careful clutch control until the very last moment, when the car should be stopped smoothly and the handbrake applied. Now select reverse gear, and again using that excellent clutch control, drive the car backwards on full left lock (first checking for safety again before letting the car move). Look over your right shoulder now, since the rear right-hand corner of the vehicle will be the nearest to the kerb. Stop again smoothly before touching the kerb; handbrake on. Select first gear, check again for safety, then move the car forward gently using clutch control and straighten the wheels in order to take up a normal cruising position in the road.

FURTHER NOTES

In the above descriptions of reversing and turning in the road, we have assumed a level surface in all cases. Your instructor will probably have a few such places marked which are suitable for early lessons. This cannot be expected to continue, though, because as you begin to make good progress he will deliberately take you to places in which it will be a little more difficult for you to carry out such manoeuvres as easily as you have been doing. The reason, of course, is that the vast majority of roads have a fairly pronounced camber in order to clear rainwater, melting snow and so on. Obviously, if you were doing the turn just described on such a road, unless you were very careful you would run too far forwards or backwards and your front or rear wheels would maybe touch the kerb on one or both sides of the road. Not for nothing have instructors named this turn the 'Three-Bump Turn'. Refer back a few paragraphs to what was said about damaging tyres. Not only is it dangerous, but it will also entail failure in the Driving Test, in which you are at the moment primarily interested. Always watch for the camber of a road, and when doing any slow manoeuvres of any kind be prepared to stop the car smoothly and apply the handbrake. When moving off, notice the gradient, and do it like a hill start. If you are always on your guard against little pitfalls of this nature it will soon become second nature to carry out the correct drill.

POINTS TO NOTE

Every time you are about to move off, use the rear-view mirror and look over your shoulder. Left shoulder if you are on the 'wrong' side of the road, and of course right shoulder under normal conditions.

Apply the handbrake first every time you bring the car to a stop, then put the gear lever into neutral.

Use the rear-view mirror every few seconds whilst driving along, and every time you intend to alter course or speed *before* signalling your intention to do so.

CHAPTER FIVE

Elementary Roadcraft

Constant practice of all primary control techniques explained in previous chapters is absolutely essential. Once steering has been mastered, anybody can just drive a car along a road, but to do so smoothly and in perfect safety is altogether another matter. Anyone who takes pride in his driving will be the first to admit that there is no such person as a perfect driver. The good, safe driver is the one who realises his own limitations and who drives with those limitations always in mind.

An example is the driver who is, perhaps, no longer in the first flush of youth. Provided he realises that his reactions are not as quick as they were a few years ago, and continually bears this in mind and allows for it, he can be just as safe a driver as anyone else on the road. Such a person will automatically adjust his speed in accordance with Highway Code rule 34 which advises one to 'always drive at such a speed that you can stop well within the distance you can see to be clear', bearing in mind that his overall stopping distance will be more than it was perhaps a decade ago. He will also adopt a greater 'hang back' distance behind the vehicle in front, for he knows that his slowing reactions will cause him to brake later than he used to do when he was younger. When the vehicle in front has to brake suddenly, he sees the brake lights come on, and has ample time to take avoiding action.

On the other hand, if this same man were to drive exactly as he was accustomed to drive, say, ten or fifteen years ago when his reactions were considerably faster, he would be a menace to himself and everybody else on the road. It would, in fact, be remarkable if he were still driving, as it is more than likely he would have had his fatal accident long ago.

Obviously, then, good driving habits should be learned from the very start, for habits are extremely hard to break and if you can once acquire good ones, you will not only become a good driver but automatically remain one. Therefore begin at this stage to try assiduously always to carry out any manoeuvre in the manner explained in previous chapters. Attention to detail is what counts most, and this is what will eventually impress the examiner when you appear at the testing centre on the Big Day.

The fact that you are now beginning to master the controls and can handle the car in a limited space does not mean that such things as preliminary checks before starting the engine, looking over one's shoulder or checking the rearview mirror, can now be omitted. They are more important than ever, because now you are about to do all these things in earnest and in actual traffic conditions. To omit any single item from the drill taught in previous chapters would at this stage be most reprehensible. At a later stage it would be both criminal and downright *dangerous*. So if you now find that you are still forgetting details of drill, however insignificant, ask your instructor to arrange for more low-speed manoeuvres in quiet roads before taking you on to busier ones.

Assuming, however, that you feel you are ready and are now getting into the swing of doing everything in the correct sequence almost automatically, let us go for an imaginary run on a road with light to medium traffic.

Having carried out preliminary checks, started the engine,

checked for safety, and moved out from the kerb, we drive along normally. There is a 'Give Way' sign ahead, so we know we are now approaching a major road. We intend to turn left on to this road, so please remember the correct drill. Mirror first, then signal for the turn, keep to the left so as to be in the correct lane for the turn, reduce speed and change down as necessary so that you will be in the correct gear if it so happens that we can go without delay. Look right, look left and look right again (if you start this before you actually get to the junction, it may not be necessary to come to a halt). If no traffic is approaching, or if it is sufficiently far away to be safe, we cross the 'Give Way' line smoothly, still keeping to the left, then accelerate and change up progressively through the gears. Now suppose there had been traffic approaching when we were coming up to that junction. We would have stopped just inside the 'Give Way' line and waited for a safe gap to appear in the line of traffic, all the time looking right, left, and right again until we decided it was safe. Then we would have moved off smoothly and smartly into the safe gap we had spotted while it was some distance away. The correct time to move the car under these circumstances is when the last car before the gap is just passing.

Pretend we have just done this. Owing to our poor acceleration (this is your first time in traffic, remember, and it is likely that you will make the beginner's mistake of being afraid of the accelerator) we have dropped too far behind the large lorry in front, so you suddenly realise this and begin to speed up. This is the time to remember the Highway Code teaching about the distance to drive behind the vehicle in front. Try not to get too close. Assuming we are in a built-up area where the speed limit is 30 mph, we should be at least 30yd behind the lorry. An easy method for estimating one's distance is to imagine the distance in bus lengths. A bus is (very approximately) about 10yd long, so at 30 mph we should obviously be roughly three bus lengths back from the lorry.

This method of estimation of distance is easy to remember, and is accepted by the examiner. All he wishes to know is that you have some idea of distance and can estimate it reasonably accurately; he is not going to fail you if you are a few feet out in your judgement. It is quite easy to imagine the requisite number of buses nose to tail, and usually much more accurate than attempting to judge the distance in yards or feet.

Remember, though, that the advice in the Highway Code applies when conditions are ideal, ie, a dry road, good visibility, good tyres on your vehicle, brakes in good condition, and the driver (you!) 100 per cent alert. If any one of those factors is below standard then the hang-back distance should be increased accordingly.

Now we are going to overtake the lorry in front.

If our hang-back distance is correct we will be able to see beyond the lorry, as shown in the diagram. (Figure 8.) If it is too close behind the lorry, then that vehicle subtends a larger angle of vision——in other words, it blocks out more of the road and we will be unable to check beyond it for safety before attempting to overtake.

DRILL FOR OVERTAKING

(i) Check that all is safe ahead and the road clear of oncoming vehicles

(ii) Use mirror to check astern that no vehicle is about to overtake our own

(iii) Signal (right flasher) that you are about to pull out

(iv) Change down to third gear (we are in a 30 mph zone, and third gear will afford greater acceleration, thus enabling us to pass faster)

(v) Use the mirror again before actually pulling out

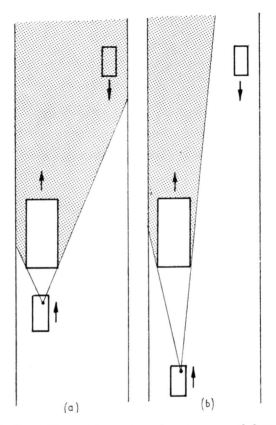

Figure 8 Overtaking: (a) car too close to rear of lorry so that oncoming vehicle is not within car driver's field of vision; (b) correct hang-back distance ensuring maximum vision ahead and oncoming car plainly visible

(vi) If still safe, accelerate hard, pulling out and passing

(vii) When clear of the overtaken vehicle, change back to top gear

(viii) Do not pull back into lane until you can see the over-taken vehicle in your rear-view mirror.

To the novice, there may seem to be quite a lot to remember in the above drill, but every step is essential.

The reason for passing as fast as possible is in order to reduce the Time Exposed to Danger (TED), which is defined as the time during which you are out of your own lane, and the reason for watching for the overtaken vehicle to appear in your rear-mirror is so that the driver of the overtaken vehicle will be able to take any avoiding action in the event of an emergency occuring. (You *could* experience a burst tyre or something equally horrifying, but you would still be sufficiently clear of him to give him a chance of avoiding you.)

ON BEING OVERTAKEN

In a previous chapter mention was made of the necessity for frequent reference to the rear-view mirror. Ideally, this should be done every few seconds in normal driving, and one should always be as much aware of the traffic picture behind as ahead. Wing mirrors help quite a lot as they reduce the blind area, and it is well worth considering having them fitted on your own car after passing the test.

Assuming that you are using the mirrors properly, you will be aware of any vehicle coming up from behind with the intention of passing you. His indicators should afford confirmation of his intention, but whether they do or not you should always be ready to anticipate his intention. Therefore hold well over to your left and let him decide when it is safe to overtake. He will do so without hesitation when he has completed his safety checks to his own satisfaction, so all you need to do is maintain a steady speed and course whilst he is passing you. The good driver is nevertheless prepared for any eventuality and you should still continue to keep a good look-out ahead and astern, so that if anything unusual occurs you will be ready to act immediately.

At this stage refer again to the Highway Code and make careful notes about what it says concerning overtaking and being overtaken. You will see a list of places and situations where overtaking must not be carried out. Remember them carefully, for not only may the examiner ask questions about them, but there is at least one very good reason for every single one of them. In many cases there are as many as six. Pause and think about each one, and try to discover the reasons behind the rules. This is what eventually makes you into a good driver. It is not enough merely to learn the rules by heart and try to remember them, because in an emergency you will not have time to ponder or search your memory for what rule so-and-so says about the situation. If you know and understand the reasons behind the rules you are very much more likely to obey them without hesitation.

We are still driving along, having overtaken a lorry and been overtaken in turn by a faster car. You are learning to use your mirror frequently. Now try not to miss any single traffic sign. From now on, whenever you are a passenger in another vehicle, exercise your observation, so that you will get into the habit of noticing every traffic sign. It goes without saying that you should by this time know all their meanings, including the road markings. If you ever see one whose meaning you do not know, make a note and look it up as soon as possible. If you put yourself to the trouble of doing things like this you will not forget them easily.

There is a side road on the left a considerable distance ahead, and we see a sportscar come hurtling along this side road towards the junction, then pull up with tyres and brakes squealing. That may be all right for him personally. Perhaps he is wealthy and can afford to wear out tyres and brakes regardless of their replacement cost. Maybe also he knows his car extremely well and can gauge just where it will come to rest when he brakes hard like that. It is still bad driving, though, and the examiner would certainly fail anyone who was foolish enough to drive like that during the test. The reason is, of course, that one should at all times have consideration for other road users, and drive accordingly. That sportscar driver did not know who was driving this car we are in—it might have been a nervous old person of either sex, who could have taken alarm at his apparent nonchalance and swerved, maybe into the path of other traffic. The sportscar driver would not have been physically involved in the resulting accident, but he most certainly would have been involved morally as a result of his flashy driving. Granted that he might be a very skilful driver, but there is a time and a place for everything. Competition driving is exhilarating, and when a certain degree of skill has been attained it is also a pleasant and satisfying pastime, but the public road is no place for it.

Whilst we are on this subject, please note that although we live in a free country and every car owner is free to decorate his vehicle in any way he sees fit, there are certain indications which, as a general rule, mark out drivers who might possibly be a risk to themselves or others. Watch for and steer well clear of: cars with masses of auxiliary lights mounted across the front; cars with 'go-faster' chequered tape stuck lavishly on them; cars with roof-mounted swivelling spotlamps; cars with mascots on the rear parcel shelf whose eyes light up when the brake pedal is pressed; cars whose drivers have not bothered to clear their rear windows of condensation, frost or snow; and cars whose side or rear windows are obscured by stickers proudly proclaiming that their owners have been to Little Puddlecombe-by-the-Sea. There are other examples, of course, but enough has been said to indicate the more common types of 'show-offs', or inconsiderate drivers.

Clean windows and clean lenses on all lights should normally mean that no other trimmings are desirable or necessary. For fast night driving or in poor visibility, one good spotlight and one good foglamp *correctly mounted* should be ample for normal use. Especially if they are quartz iodine or quartz halogen types, which provide much more brilliant illumination than the older types of auxiliary lamps. And always bear in mind that while on the public roads an uneventful drive is a good drive. The best drivers are unassuming, courteous, observant and alert; the bad ones merely struggle along from incident to incident.

Now in this imaginary drive we have covered barely a mile so far, but this first time out on a major road has brought up a number of very important points. Let us now pull in at the side of the road and reconsider all that has been discussed above.

Remember the drill: first select a safe spot at which to pull in. Now use the mirror before starting to apply the foot-brake. Use it lightly several times so that the brake lights flash intermittently and draw the attention of following traffic to the fact that we intend to slow down and stop. Now, firm progressive braking as we glide in to the selected spot. Now we have stopped, so apply the handbrake, select neutral and then switch off the engine. Notice that all these things were still carried out in the correct sequence despite the fact that you were doing them in an unfamiliar situation.

In this chapter we have considered a straightforward drive just a short distance along a major road, and in the course of it several points have emerged which are new to the novice driver. The most important of these is perhaps behaviour at and near junctions. The examiners are particularly watchful of your behaviour at junctions and crossroads, and the following are the main points for which they watch.

BEHAVIOUR AT JUNCTIONS AND CROSSROADS

(i) Regulate your speed of approach, changing gear as necessary

(ii) Use the rear-view mirror

(iii) Signal your intentions if you are going to turn

(iv) Stop if necessary

(v) Look right, left and right again *before* emerging
(vi) Emerge with due regard to approaching traffic
(vii) Pick up the speed of the traffic on the road you have joined—smoothly.

Now read this chapter again slowly and analyse the reasons behind the points enumerated under 'Drill for Overtaking' and 'Behaviour at Junctions and Crossroads'. Ask yourself if you understand the logic behind the sequence in which they are arranged. Try to remember that sequence, and if you can put it into practice the next time you have a lesson in the car with your instructor, he will be delighted at the progress you are making.

PRACTICE

At this stage we can usefully consider the correct method of parking a car parallel to the kerb. Many people just drive in headfirst, regardless of whether the car is going to fit reasonably well into the vacant space. This, of course, results in the stern of the car sticking out into the road and causing a hazard to traffic on the same side. Quite apart from thus endangering your own car, the hazard it may present to other traffic could at the least cause congestion and at the worst an accident as the result of other traffic swerving to avoid it.

The correct method, although it calls for a certain amount of initial caution, results in a properly and neatly parked vehicle which is already poised to drive straight out again when you have completed the visit for which you found it necessary to park. (See Figure 9.)

Drive just past the car ahead of the space you have selected, so that your passenger's front door is level with the stationary car's front wing. (In all these manoeuvres you should first use the mirror and signal your intention to slow down or stop before touching the brakes.)

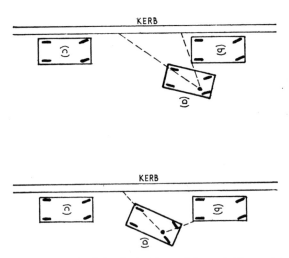

Figure 9 Correct method for kerbside parking: (*left*) car (a) has just started to reverse, aiming his rear nearside wheel at centre of space between (b) and (c); (*right*) just as (a)'s nearside front wheel comes level with (b)'s offside rear wing, (a) swing his steering wheel to full right lock, bringing the front of his car in towards the kerb and preventing the rear wheel riding over it

Now start to reverse straight back very slowly. As the nearside rear wing of your car comes level with the offside rear wing of the stationary car behind which you are going to park, start to turn the steering wheel to your left in order to aim the centre of the rear of your own vehicle at the kerb roughly midway between the two cars ahead and astern of you. (See Figure 10.) Continue to proceed slowly backwards, at the same time transferring your attention to the nearside front wing of your own car. As this just begins to clear the rear offside wing of the car in front, quickly swing the steering wheel hard to the right, thus bringing the front of your own car sharply inwards. The moment you are satisfied that you are clear of the car in front, look to the rear again in order to ensure that you do not touch the car behind you. If you have judged matters correctly you should now be parked neatly between the car in front and the one behind, with your front wheels on right lock ready to drive out. Apply handbrake and switch off engine. This exercise, although not required at present in the Driving Test, is excellent for the development of judgement and clutch control, and should be used on every possible occasion.

Figure 10   This is what it looks like to a bystander

HELPFUL HINTS

1   When you start a cold engine, do not let it idle too long. Drive away as soon as possible; this minimises engine wear.

2   Naturally, you have to sometimes slip the clutch a bit—pulling away, reversing, parking and so on, but when doing so never race the engine or you will burn the clutch lining and maybe crack the pressure plate.

3   Too much acceleration when starting from rest only burns petrol, wears out tyres and ruins the suspension. Anyway, all you would save would be seconds.

4   Modern cars with their light flywheels and high-revving engines are not designed for high-gear starting, so never move off in second gear or the clutch will suffer.

5   Keep engine revs down until normal running temperature has been reached.

6   Over-enthusiastic cornering can not only induce skids, it can mean an early grave for your tyres.

7   In order to keep the windscreen clear of scratches, never use the wipers on a dry screen. Always press the washer button first.

8   Don't ever slog the engine. Always match the gear to the speed.

9   The quickest way to ruin the clutch is to rest your foot on the pedal whilst driving.

10 Early braking means lighter braking, and saves wear on brake linings and tyres. Late braking induces skids and causes accidents.

11 Avoid touching kerbs if you wish your tyres to remain safe.

12 Always apply the handbrake *after* the car stops, or only the rear brakes will be doing all the work, and this also induces skids.

13 Squeeze the handbrake button when applying it as well as when releasing it. If you acquire the bad habit of ignoring this button the handbrake makes a horrible noise and the ratchet wears rapidly. Then will come the day when it won't hold the car on an incline.

14 Don't ever turn the steering wheel unless the car is moving or the front wheels are jacked up. This is to save excessive wear on both tyres and steering mechanism.

15 Remember that any unusual noise is often an early warning of something loose, worn or out of adjustment. Trace every noise as soon as it is noted, and find out its cause. With cars, it could prove fatal to yourself or others to put off until tomorrow what should be done NOW.

CHAPTER SIX

Everyday Driving

The professional driver is out on the road in almost all conditions throughout the year, so that summer or winter conditions mean for him only that he has to change his driving technique accordingly. Unfortunately this is by no means the case with less experienced drivers. With them, deteriorating conditions generally mean the fear of an unexpected skid and uncertainty about what one should do if one occurs, or if visibility decreases. There should be no reason for this dread, provided one thinks ahead and uses a modicum of commonsense.

Skid conditions, for instance, do not occur only in winter. At any time of the year, if it has been dry for several days or maybe weeks, a sudden shower of rain can induce very treacherous conditions indeed even on good roads. During the dry weather a deposit of oily drips and splashes accumulates, mixed with a thin film of tyre rubber. As soon as it rains, this mass at once becomes like a skating rink. A scattering of autumn leaves made wet by rain is another hazard, and so, too, is any layer of loose gravel, partly repaired roads and so on. All these are perhaps even more dangerous than the dreaded snow or ice, for one can usually see or feel that it is snowing or freezing. The other conditions are more dangerous because they are much more subtle and less easily recognised.

Before discussing skids, let us for a moment consider the forces which act upon a car. A vehicle in motion normally tends to travel in a straight line, and one has to turn the wheels deliberately in order to steer it around a bend or corner. When the wheels of a car are misaligned, as in a corner, the car is not in a stable condition and if speed is too high a skid of some kind will result. In a bend, centrifugal force acts on any vehicle, as you can readily feel for yourself when your body tends to sway outwards. Careless driving will exaggerate these conditions and result in one of the following three basic types of skid.

FOUR-WHEEL SKID

Imagine poor road conditions. You are travelling much too close to the vehicle in front when you suddenly see his brake lights come on. In a panic, you brake and, because you are too close, you brake rather too hard. Your wheels will lock more easily than usual because of the poor grip offered by the slippery road surface. The car will now slide in a straight line, and if there is the slightest downhill gradient will actually pick up speed. You will therefore hit the car in front with a resounding thud, resulting in extensive damage and probable injury. There is seldom room to avoid him by steering, and in any case that type of avoiding action would probably, on this surface, have resulted in a more complex skid and multi-vehicular damage. So what is one to do?

Prevention being a thousand times better than cure, the simple answer is to drive always at a distance far enough back from the vehicle in front to be able to stop within the distance you can see to be clear. (Para 35 of the Highway Code again.) The above situation would not then arise.

Supposing, however, that it did (owing to your momentary

66

inattention, perhaps), then all is not irretrievably lost. Remember that the maximum braking effect on wheels occurs *just before* those wheels lock. Release your brakes and brake again quickly. In other words 'pump' your brake pedal. This will result in a series of applications of the maximum braking effect on all wheels, and is technically known as 'cadence' braking. It may not actually prevent you hitting the car in front, but it will undoubtedly reduce the force of the impact and may make all the difference between broken necks and broken lamp-glasses. The accident would, of course, have been your fault, for a driver's first duty is to avoid the danger in front of him. Even if the car in front had braked to avoid a careless pedestrian, you should still have been observing para 35 of the Code.

REAR-WHEEL SKID

This time you are approaching, let us say, a right-hand bend in potential skid conditions, but your speed is more appropriate to perfect summer (dry) roads. As the car enters the bend you feel the rear end begin to swing outwards. What has happened is that centrifugal force is acting on the whole car to try to force it outwards towards the left-hand verge, but because the front of the car, with the engine, gearbox, battery, driver and so on, is very much heavier than the rear end, the front wheels are pressed down more firmly upon the road, giving the front of the car a very much better grip of the surface than the rear end. The rear wheels therefore slide sideways. The reason for the skid was that there was too much speed in the wrong place. Now the very first thing to do in a skid is to remove its cause—so foot *off* the accelerator smartly, but *do not brake* or you will complicate the situation. Engine revs will immediately begin to drop and the car will start to lose speed. Now correct by steering. There is no need to say any more than that, for the steering will be instinctive. Some people will tell you to 'steer into the skid', which is, of course, correct but I prefer to merely tell you not to overdo the steering correction, or you will induce a rather more complex situation.

FRONT-WHEEL SKID

Now let us imagine the same situation which led to the skid in the above paragraph. This time, though, as you enter the bend and turn the wheel slightly to the right to take the car round the bend, you are horrified to find that it continues to travel in a straight line. What has happened is that you have turned the front wheels, but they have, in the poor gripping conditions offered by the road surface, failed to do their job properly, with the result that they are actually sliding sideways. Should this occur, there is only one remedy, and it takes quite a bit of courage. Remove the cause of the skid (too much speed) as above, then straighten the wheels and try again as the car's speed drops. You will by now have realised that if you let any of these conditions occur you will probably half scare yourself to death. Therefore resolve always to drive so that skids are least likely to happen.

Much more important than learning how to control skids is to drive so that they will not take you unawares. This is obviously achieved by first realising that skid conditions are, in fact, present, and then merely doing what your instinct and good sense dictates—ie, never accelerate or brake violently; approach bends and corners with circumspection, and adopt a longer 'hang-back' position than you do in dry conditions. In other words, drive as you would walk upon a sheet of ice.

Only the simplest types of skid have been dealt with. There are others of a more complex nature, but it is unlikely that you will ever meet with them unless you decide to take up competition driving. This can involve the deliberate use of controlled skids, such as handbrake turns, in rallies or on the driving tests usually associated with them, or perhaps four-wheel drifts in racing, but by the time you are doing this kind of thing you will not need to read books about it. Here it is only necessary to say that they are definitely *not* for normal driving on the Queen's highway and could lead to charges of dangerous driving at the very least. If you do ever take up competition driving, practice upon a proper skid-pan is desirable and should preferably be carried out under skilled instruction at first. It is good fun—after the first fifteen minutes or so!

FORDS AND FLOODS

Sudden heavy rain can produce flooding in many parts of the country at almost any time of the year, and drivers who are fond of using minor roads and country lanes are likely to find fords or watersplashes to be negotiated. The accepted method is to reduce speed considerably, change to a low gear and try to proceed slowly through what looks like the shallow-est part (usually the crown of the road) so that your passage does not splash water into the engine compartment and the engine is ticking over fast enough to prevent the ingress of water at the exhaust pipe, which could result in back pressure and stop the engine. When the car is clear of the water and has climbed the far bank (if any), it is wise to test the brakes as soon as convenient, for soaked brakes will be inefficient. If they are not as effective as usual, then drive for a short distance with one foot lightly on the brake; the heat generated will very soon dry them out.

Should you be unlucky enough to get into deeper water than expected, or to stop your engine through drenching the electrical system, the car may still be driven out on the starter motor using the lowest gear. When on dry ground, you can then dry out the electrical system, paying particular attention to the sparking plugs and their leads, the coil, and the inside of the distributor cap. When these are thoroughly dry you should be able to restart, provided you have not exhausted the battery whilst getting the car ashore. In this event, it might still be possible to restart with the aid of a push or a tow.

Once a driver is aware of potentially hazardous conditions and feels that he knows how to tackle them, he has little to worry about apart from fog.

DRIVING IN FOG

A motorway patrol officer once told me that the police wished they knew what it was that causes driver to 'belt on regardless' in fog conditions. He mentioned a case where there was a grass fire at the side of the road and the wind was blowing dense smoke across both carriageways. This could be seen the best part of a mile away, but nevertheless drivers still hurtled into it at speeds of 60 and 70 mph. The result was a thirty-car smash-up, and they had to visit three separate hospitals to get statements from the victims.

In very dense fog, which is really a dense mist, there are certain precautions which anyone can take, and these are all based on sound commonsense. Perhaps one day there will be some form of radar to assist fog driving, but this is not yet in sight and meanwhile the authorities are doing their best by erecting crash barriers on motorways and trunk roads at places known to have a high accident rate. They are also installing suitable overhead lighting as fast as possible where necessary. It is up to the motorist to co-operate as best he can by fitting good quality foglamps with a sharp cutoff at the top of the beam. The quartz iodine (Q.I.) variety afford the best illumination, and the nearside lamp should be aimed at the kerb. Do not follow this too slavishly, though, or you may end up in somebody's front drive, or on some road other than the one you want. N.B. NEVER use single lights.

FOG CODE

1 Slow down; keep a safe distance. You should always be able to pull up within your range of vision.

2 Don't hang on to someone else's tail lights; it gives you a false sense of security.

3 Watch your speed; you may be going much faster than you think.

4 Remember that if you are in a heavy vehicle you need a good deal longer to pull up.

5 Warning signals are there to help and protect. Do observe them.

6 See and be seen—use headlights or fog lamps.

7 Check and clean windscreen, lights, reflectors and windows whenever you can.

8 If you must drive in fog, allow more time for your journey.

The Fog Code, drawn up by Mr John Peyton, when Minister for Transport Industries, in an effort to minimise motorway pile-ups in fog

The increasing tendency for some local authorities to skimp on the catseyes is to be deprecated. Maybe they find that white paint is cheaper, but it does not save as many lives as those dear old catseyes which are so very welcome when the tired driver is groping his way homewards in atrocious visibility. A very good idea is to open your windows and turn off the car radio, for that helps to identify and locate other traffic by sound. Remember an old sailor's tip and notice the bearing of any light you may sight; if that bearing does not alter, then you are on a collision course and need to do something fast.

Another point to watch is that, if you are leading a queue, your car will cleave some sort of vague clearance through the fog and this may lull following drivers into a false sense of security. One of them may become impatient at what he considers to be your partial blindness and incompetence, and try to overtake you. There is nothing much you can do about this except to be aware of this possibility and to let him do so safely. Let him take his turn at pathfinding. Be very careful, though, when he is passing you, for he may not have realised that it is quite so dense ahead and may try to pull back in again. So long as you are aware of the possibility you will be able to let him in safely. If he does pass, then follow *well back*, mentally wishing him good luck.

At the very last resort, when the fog is so thick that you can barely see the end of your own bonnet, get somebody to walk ahead with a flashlamp, aiming it either downwards at his own feet or at the kerb just ahead of you.

Roads and vehicles are improving all the time, and to say that a road or a vehicle was responsible for a collision means that the vehicle was being driven in a manner which was unsafe for that particular situation, or for the characteristics of that particular vehicle in those conditions, or that it was poorly maintained. Nevertheless, there are certain drivers who use the roads badly and others who use them correctly and well. A minority of drivers have a congenital urge to take risks for the sake of taking them, and half your battle as a driver is to be able to recognise such drivers and steer well clear of them because these are the people who cause the crashes in conditions of poor visibility or bad weather. Keep well astern of them.

All major car manufacturers are going very seriously into the question of safety for the occupants of vehicles in the event of a collision. A car incorporating all their recommendations would be far beyond the means of most people but at least all cars now have seat belts as a standard fitting, unless they were registered before the law was introduced, and they should be worn on every occasion that the car is used.

When summer arrives, do not become too complacent, because it has its own peculiarities for the motorist. Fast driving on a lovely summer afternoon or evening is almost guaranteed to cover your windscreen with a sludge of slaughtered insects, and oil fumes from other traffic seem to have some sort of affinity with this goo, turning it into a revolting paste. Fortunately, the manufacturers of car chemicals are one up here and market little sachets of preparations which you add to the water in the washer reservoir. This can clean your screen in a few seconds.

As well as dangerous conditions, there are dangerous times as well. No doubt you will be able to think of several in your own district. Rush hours, when people hurry to and from work; school times, with children hurrying so as not to be late; lunch hour with its jaywalkers; pub-crawlers in the early evening, followed by closing time when there is a general exodus from the houses of good cheer. This used to be the peak accident time of the whole 24 hours until the introduction of the present breathalyser laws.

Many instructors do not mention anything about driving under adverse conditions, sometimes because they do not wish to frighten you, but more often because they are concentrating on preparing you for the Driving Test. Bear in mind that the test was introduced in 1935 and has hardly changed since then despite the fact that traffic density has increased out of all proportion, vehicle performance has improved in a spectacular fashion, road conditions in general are completely different, and situations arise today which could not possibly have been forseen some forty-odd years ago. The only thing, so far as the test is concerned, that has changed is that the examiners have received instructions to implement their terms of reference more meticulously. This only means that you will find it a little more difficult to pass the test than someone who took it, say twenty years ago. If you religiously follow the advice in this book, however, there is no reason whatever why you should doubt the outcome of the test. Provided you have practised regularly and sufficiently, you will have an excellent chance of success.

The Royal Automobile Club is one of the most active organisations concerned with driving instruction, and when a pupil passes his test after having received instruction from a RAC Registered Instructor he may enter the following year for the L Driver of the Year Competition, the 'star' prize for which is generally a brand new car. Further details of this competition and of the special tests it involves may be obtained on application to the Royal Automobile Club, Pall Mall, London, S.W.1, or from any RAC Registered Instructor.

The competition provides valuable experience and will appeal particularly to those drivers who, though they have passed the test, realise that they still have a great deal to learn. The newly-qualified driver has, after all, had no tuition at all on actual motorways, often he has never driven at night, it is very unlikely that he has ever driven in really bad conditions, like ice or snow, and certainly not in fog. He has probably never driven in heavy traffic or experienced a skid—even on a skidpan, yet he has passed the 'test of competence to drive a motorcar'! Driving schools and examiners are by no means at fault. It is the system which leaves a great deal to be desired.

For these reasons the novice driver would be very well advised, after passing his test, to enrol for a further short series of lessons, during which motorway driving could be introduced and, if possible, bad weather and night driving as well as driving in heavy traffic on, perhaps, a Saturday morning in a large city. Obviously these extra lessons will cost more money, and driving lessons are becoming more expensive all the time, but they will still be an excellent investment when set against the expense which could result from an accident which should never happen to a driver with sufficient experience. That is the one thing which you now

lack, and nothing can take the place of experience and practice. Ideally, the Driving Test should be taken about half-way
through a properly-designed driving course, after which the
successful pupil could go ahead in the sure knowledge that
real progress was being made and with his mind free to concentrate on learning to drive properly.

It was mentioned in a previous chapter that good habits
were hard to eliminate, and that assiduous practice was the
only way in which to implant them. Some of these good
habits have already been mentioned, such as looking in your
mirror and checking over your shoulder before permitting
the car to move, using the mirror before any alteration of
course or speed, or before signalling your intention of carrying out any manoeuvre, checking ahead and astern carefully
before reversing, and so on. These are, after all, commonsense precautions and should by this time become almost
second nature to you. There are, however, a few other things
which are perhaps not quite so obvious to the novice driver,
but should also be done automatically when necessary. The
following are a few examples.

PARKING ON A HILL

You will remember it was explained in Chapter 1 that the
handbrake acts only on the rear wheels and is not, therefore,
so effective as the footbrake, which acts on all four wheels.
Obviously, then, if we park the car on a fairly steep hill and
there is the slightest thing wrong with the handbrake system
(such as a stretched cable, unevenly adjusted brake pressure,
or a worn handbrake ratchet), the car could be caused to roll
when unattended. Have you noticed how the slipstream from
a passing lorry can rock a car? The modern car is usually
fairly heavy and, given a start, will soon pick up some speed
on a hill, from which damage, injury, or even death could
result. You, as the driver, could be responsible, even though

you were not actually in the car at the time, because you had parked it in that position. If you are aware of the possibility, no accident need occur, for there are no less than three separate precautions one can take in order to prevent a car from rolling away from its parking spot on a hill. Here they are: (i) The handbrake (already mentioned many times); (ii) the gears; if the car is facing downhill, leave it in reverse gear, and if uphill in first gear; (iii) steering: if the car is facing downhill, turn the wheels in towards the kerb; if facing uphill, turn them outwards.

Now pause a moment and consider the result of these precautions singly. Think what would happen if the car began to roll if any two of the three safety measures had been applied. Sometimes there is no kerb, and it is then possible only to take two out of the three precautions. Nevertheless, one should get into the habit of taking at least two of them every time one stops the car on a hill. There is absolutely no excuse for the cases which are occasionally reported in the press describing, say, a lorry running down a hill unattended and out of control and perhaps killing a baby in a parked pram. When interviewed, the driver usually says, 'The handbrake must have failed!' whereas, in fact, in the majority of cases, it is likely to have been due to his own criminal negligence.

USE OF HEADLIGHTS

In the country at night always keep headlights on and use your discretion as to when they should be dipped or on main beam. Do not be tempted to use only sidelights when following other cars. You would then be less visible, and could even be wrongly identified (maybe as a bicycle, by somebody who could see only one of your sidelights), also your vision would be greatly reduced. Maybe in a crawling traffic queue it would be safe to use sidelights only and also less likely to inconvenience the driver ahead of you.

In town, use headlights always unless the street lighting is exceptional. Remember the recommendations of the Highway Code, and keep them dipped in built-up areas. It is much easier for other road-users to spot a car driving along on dipped headlights than one which is on sidelights—particularly on a rainy night when reflections are everywhere.

It is good manners to dip your headlights when driving behind another car, and also in the face of oncoming traffic. If somebody dazzles you by failing to dip, try not to become annoyed. Slow down, and stop if necessary. The driver behind you will understand, for he will also be suffering from the unthinking moron who is approaching in a blinding glare of light. The one single danger is that the car behind may be dazzled to such an extent that he may be unable to see you slowing down or stopping, and run into you. Of course that would be his fault, for the courts have consistently maintained that a driver's first duty is to avoid the danger in front of him. Besides, he should have been travelling at such a speed that he could have stopped within the distance he could see to be clear. Also, that kind of collision is infinitely preferable to a head-on one with the oncoming car, especially as a driver insensitive enough to drive towards you with his headlights blazing is also likely to be driving at an excessive speed. This is an instance of where one deliberately selects the lesser of two evils.

TYRE TROUBLES

Even though tyre pressures are checked regularly, as previously recommended, there is always the possibility of a puncture or a burst. Punctures are more annoying than dangerous because you will usually get some sort of warning that a tyre is going flat; wandering or heavy steering, a bumpy ride on what appears to be a smooth road, or a general unbalance of the car, steadily becoming worse.

Bursts are quite another kettle of fish and generally happen quite suddenly with the car trying to swerve. Do not panic on any account, but use your strength to try to hold the car in a straight line. Below about 30 mph a burst is not often a very serious matter and is easy to control; above, say about 40 mph, it can be rather frightening and you may have to battle hard with the steering to avoid a collision or to prevent the car from leaving the road.

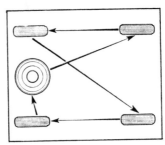

Figure 11 Illustrating the recommended method of changing tyres around in order to obtain even wear. It also means you will eventually have to replace all tyres more or less at the same time. An alternative is to change only front wheels and rear wheels with their opposite numbers. Then, whichever pair first shows excessive wear, you replace them by the spare and one new tyre, retaining the best of the discarded pair as a spare

As always, prevention is better than cure, so see that your tyres are kept in good condition. Be careful to avoid striking the kerb with them, and if you are unfortunate enough to do so, then use that tyre only as a spare in future. By doing this you are at least reducing the likelihood of a burst. Also remember to change the tyres around at intervals to obtain even wear. (See Figure 11.)

AQUAPLANING

There is one type of 'skid' (not really a skid) which has not yet been mentioned. Just as a water skier skims over the

78

surface at speed but sinks when his speed is reduced, so a car can behave in a similar fashion. If the surface of the road is very wet indeed, the grip of the wheels on the road can progressively lessen until, instead of there being any traction, the wheels are actually skimming along on a sort of microfilm of water. This is most likely to happen at speeds of about 60 mph or above, and the car *may* continue in a reasonably straight line. Do not count on this, though, for the slightest side wind, bump in the road, steering movement or braking could induce a rather hair-raising slide—in an almost unpredictable direction. The moral here is, when in doubt, reduce speed. Commonsense again.

ECONOMY

With the ever-increasing cost of petrol and oil it makes sense to drive in such a way that your fuel bills will not be larger than absolutely necessary. There are also several other steps which can be taken to reduce petrol consumption. You can, if you wish, and have some mechanical skill, try to achieve economy by tuning your carburettor(s); this involves changing the jet(s)—so that a weaker mixture is fed to the cylinders, or perhaps varying the size of the choke tube. Both methods are a bit disappointing, for although you may perhaps gain a mile or two per gallon it will be at the expense of your car's performance. After all, the designer of your engine has already established optimum figures for such things, and since he has been doing this for very much longer than you your best bet is to leave well alone. But there are quite a few other steps that can be taken without fiddling with carburettors, or indeed anything else.

Here are a few obvious ones:

(i) Check the petrol system throughout for leaks, and cure any you find.

(ii) Ensure that the air cleaner is itself clean. If it is not in pristine condition it will, of course, restrict the flow of air drawn in by the carburettor and cause the mixture to be too rich, ie, the ratio of petrol to air will be too high. Make certain, too, that the filter element in the petrol pump is also clean. (See Figure 12.)

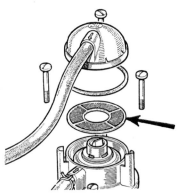

Figure 12   The filter element (arrowed) in a mechanical petrol pump should be checked to ensure it is not blocked by sludge resulting from lack of maintenance

(iii) Periodically check for wear at the carburettor needle valve, throttle spindle bearings, and see that the float is not punctured, for that would cause flooding. If you are uncertain about how to go about checking these, any reputable garage will do it for you, and it is one of those jobs well worth paying to have done by an expert.

(iv) Ensure that the engine and transmission are in tip-top condition, for if things are getting to the stage where the car is no longer as lively as it once was, it is going to cost you more in petrol and oil than it previously did. Better to spend a few pounds and get it put right than waste perhaps hundreds in the long run. Maybe it only needs decarbonisation anyway.

(v) Check all tyre pressures regularly. This makes good sense in the light of what you have already read about skids, bursts and the law. Moreover, if your tyres are underinflated, not only are the tyres themselves going to suffer from undue flexing of the sidewalls with consequent overheating, but they will offer more surface area to the ground, so that additional tractive effort will be necessary with consequent wastage of fuel.

(vi) On starting from cold, use the choke for the minimum possible time. An engine running with an over-rich mixture is a foul engine from all points of view, as well as wasting expensive fuel.

(vii) Drive intelligently. This includes all the above but also means intelligent anticipation of road and traffic conditions. Do not always just drive on regardless; try to achieve the maximum benefit from your observations ahead. You will soon develop a sort of sixth sense which will serve as a kind of early warning system so that you will be ready, almost without realising it, when the other person sharing the road with you starts to do something silly.

Everybody has two main divisions in their brain; the conscious and the subconscious. The conscious portion is that which takes care of all non-routine matters such as deteriorating weather conditions, variations of traffic conditions and so on. The subconscious portion instinctively demands changes of speed, and even calls for subtle alterations of course. For it to work effectively while driving, the mind should be kept clear of distractions. If somebody tries to start a serious conversation, by all means be polite, but postpone full participation in it until a more appropriate time and place. If you join in, then not only will your petrol consumption suffer, but other things as well. Suppose you are chatting merrily away whilst approaching traffic lights. Suddenly you realise they are changing to red, and you brake too hard and too late. You have not only used some extra petrol by holding your speed too long, but you have also worn the brakes and tyres more than necessary as well as perhaps giving the driver of the car behind you a bit of a fright. Good, considerate driving and economy driving have a great deal in common.

Reverting to the fuel crisis, one other matter might with advantage be mentioned here. Buying petrol was not so easy for the early motorists as it still is for us today, for only scattered shops stocked 'petroleum spirit', and some motorists made the mistake of asking for 'petroleum oil', which is really paraffin. If they had sufficient petrol in their tanks already, the motor would run; if not, they used to wonder why it would not start. Remembering this, some people in World War II managed to run their cars on a mixture of petrol and paraffin. Modern car engines are, as a rule, of a much higher compression ratio than those which were built before the war, and as a result are even less likely to run on a paraffin cocktail. In any case, do not try it, for it is false economy and could ruin your engine. Also it causes additional pollution, and is quite illegal.

IMPORTANT CAUTION

Many of the more popular cars are today fitted with a security device known as a 'steering column lock'. There are drivers who try to economise on fuel by changing into neutral and switching off their engines, thus causing the vehicle to free-wheel or 'coast' down hills. In itself, this is a reprehensible practice, since, with the engine switched off, you not only have no engine braking power available but cannot accelerate out of trouble.

Where a steering column lock is involved, the situation is very much worse, because when such a lock is used for the purpose of switching off the engine it becomes impossible to steer the car at all. So make very certain that if you are driving such a car you do not switch off the engine *ever* whilst the car is moving. Better still—get into the habit of regarding coasting as a downright dangerous practice.

CHAPTER SEVEN

How a Car Works

During this century the motorcar has evolved from a freakish invention into a highly sophisticated means of transport, and as its design has become ever more complicated so have its handling and maintenance increased in complexity. However, if one considers it piecemeal, the apparent complexity begins to resolve itself into a logical sequence, and one's understanding of the whole machine is simplified.

A car can be divided conveniently into the following sections for the purpose of this chapter: (i) engine; (ii) transmission; (iii) wheels, brakes and tyres; (iv) electrical system; (v) body and trimmings.

The engines in use on today's cars are mainly petrol-driven, although there are indications that as a result of the increasing world shortage of oil cars relying upon other forms of motive power may possibly be introduced in the foreseeable future, especially as the large motor manufacturers have been carrying out a considerable amount of development work in this field for the past few years.

THE ENGINE

If a container is fiilled with a mixture of petrol and air, then compressed and fired by an electric spark, the container would certainly burst. Here, then, is a potential source of great energy, and the petrol engine is merely a properly designed device for the control and effective use of this energy.

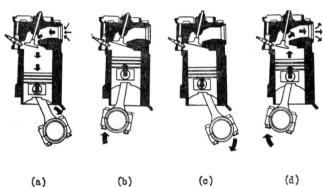

(a)　　　　(b)　　　　(c)　　　　(d)

Figure 13　The four-stroke petrol engine: (a) the 'induction' stroke; (b) the 'compression' stroke; (c) the 'ignition' stroke and (d) the 'exhaust' stroke. In this much simplified drawing, the same valve is shown dealing with both inlet and exhaust gases whereas, in practice, there are at least two to each cylinder. The crank portion for this cylinder would follow the path indicated by the heavy arrows at the bottom

Figure 13 shows a cylinder containing a piston which is allowed to slide up and down inside it. This piston is linked to a crankshaft by means of a connecting rod. The crankshaft is made to turn in the same way as the crankshaft of a bicycle is made to turn by the motion of one's legs. For the legs, substitute the connecting rod of the petrol engine, and you will get the idea of how the 'up and down' motion is converted into a rotary motion in order to, eventually, drive the wheels of the car.

Of course there is a bit more to it than this. Petrol has to be allowed into the cylinder, and burnt gases (exhaust)

allowed to escape on each sequence. To provide for this, the cylinder has to have inlet and outlet 'ports' cut in its head, and these have to be opened and closed by means of valves. These valves, in turn, have to have some form of mechanism which is able to open and close them at the appropriate times, and these times must be absolutely precise. It is rational, therefore, to use the same cycle of events to control these valves as is used to turn the crankshaft, or alternatively to use the crankshaft itself to drive the 'camshaft', which is the gadget that operates the inlet and outlet valves of the cylinder head.

Look at Figure 13 and imagine that the crankshaft is being turned slowly by hand. As the piston descends, a charge of air (mixed with petrol) will be drawn into the cylinder; this is the 'induction' stroke shown at (a) in a simplified form. When the crankshaft continues to rotate, the piston will reach the bottom of its stroke and begin to rise in the cylinder. By this time the inlet valve has closed, and the explosive mixture is therefore beginning to be compressed as the piston rises and reduces the area of the 'compression chamber', where the sparking plug lurks, ready to produce a spark sufficient to cause the mixture to fire. The increasing compression in the combustion chamber causes any suspended droplets of petrol to be vaporised, and thus rendered even more explosive.

Almost at the end of the compression stroke (b), a spark occurs between the electrodes of the sparking plug, which fires the mixture, causing an extremely sharp pressure rise. The force of this pressure causes the 'firing stroke' and firmly forces the piston downwards again (c). Now that the engine has 'fired', it will continue to operate under its own power. Near the end of the firing stroke the exhaust valve will open and permit the escape of the waste gases from the combustion chamber as the momentum of the flywheel causes the crankshaft to continue to revolve and consequently force the piston upwards again within the cylinder (d). This upwards movement forces the burned gases out of the cylinder in order to leave it free for the incoming petrol and air mixture on the following induction stroke. The operation of this form of engine, known as a four-stroke engine, is summarised by apprentice mechanics as 'Suck, Squeeze, Bang, Blow', corresponding to the (a), (b), (c) and (d) of the illustration.

Some cars operate on a two-stroke cycle, but the four-stroke engine is much more common. It is called a four-stroke engine because power is transmitted to the crankshaft only on every fourth stroke of the piston, as we have seen. Naturally, if only one piston were to be used, the engine would run in a jerky fashion, and for this reason it is usual to have a number of cylinders, each containing the same, or a similar arrangement to that shown diagrammatically above; hence we have varying engine arrangements such as four-cylinder, six-cylinder, eight-cylinder and so on. The cylinders themselves can be either arranged in a straight line, horizontally opposed, or set in a 'V' formation, and so on. Generally speaking, the more cylinders, the smoother the engine runs. Unfortunately, one never gets something for nothing, so that as a general rule the larger the engine, the more fuel it will use and the more it will cost to run. Also, more complex machinery has a larger fault potential. Hence the popularity of four-stroke four cylinder 'in line' engines.

In the above discussion it was mentioned that a petrol and air mixture had to be caused to enter the cylinder before the engine could work. The component which determines the correct mixture of petrol to air is called the carburettor. A mixture containing too much air in relation to petrol is called a 'weak' mixture, and of course a 'rich' mixture means one which is over-rich in petrol. In order that the engine should run satisfactorily and economically the mixture must be correct—neither too weak nor too rich.

Basically, all carburettors store a small quantity of petrol in a 'float chamber'; this is so designed that it maintains a constant level, the float causing a valve to open and admit more petrol when the level falls. When it rises, of course, the float rises with it and so causes the valve to shut. In this way the level is kept fairly constant. The petrol outlet to the engine is located in the 'throat' of the carburettor and is called the 'jet'. The size of this jet fixes the rate of flow of the petrol for a given amount of air flow, and if the jet size is correct the strength of the mixture will also be correct and the engine will run smoothly and economically. There is also a valve in the inlet pipe known as the 'throttle valve', which is used to control the power delivered by the engine. It does this by merely acting as an obstruction between the outside atmosphere and the cylinders of the engine. Briefly, this is all that you need to know about the operation of a carburettor. Their adjustment is usually a matter for experts, and meddling with mixture strength is not to be recommended.

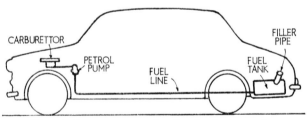

Figure 14 The fuel system: as the level of the carburettor in a modern car is usually above that of the petrol tank, a mechanical or electric pump is usually incorporated to raise the fuel to the height of the mixture intake

Figure 14 shows the layout of a typical fuel system in a conventional front-engine rear-wheel drive car. In other types the actual components making up the system may be differently located, ie, in a transverse-engined car the petrol pump and carburettor may be in another position, although they will be still at the front of the car. In some the petrol pump may be at the rear near the tank. In a rear-engined car the location may be different again. The general principle, though, is always the same; a tank to hold the fuel, a pump to raise it to the level of the carburettor and the carburettor itself mounted on a manifold which enables it to feed the mixture into the engine.

Figure 15 illustrates a simple method of foiling any attempt by thieves to siphon petrol from tanks of unattended cars—an ever-present risk in times of fuel shortage.

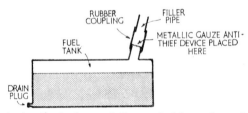

Figure 15   A simple device to foil petrol thieves is a piece of metal gauze inserted in the position shown

THE TRANSMISSION

Since an internal combustion engine is unable to produce any torque (turning force) unless it is turning at several hundred revolutions per minute, it becomes necessary to provide some means of isolating the engine from the remainder of the mechanism so that the engine may be started in the first place. This is where the clutch comes in. It is also, as was explained in Chapter 2, necessary for the purpose of disconnecting the engine from the gearbox during the operation of changing from one gear to another. Also, if the gears are completely disengaged (neutral), the engine is then mechanically free and may be started and allowed to idle whilst the car itself remains at rest. Most cars use a friction type of clutch; the type which was referred to in Chapter 2. Of course, it would be possible to construct all the portions of the assembly separately and then link them up mechanically, but modern practice dictates that engine, clutch housing and gearbox be connected together rigidly and mounted on the car as a unit. This can lead to a compact design, and with modern materials becoming lighter all the time, the necessity for a flexible coupling of some kind between the clutch and the gearbox is eliminated. Also alignment is made precise. The main difference between an actual clutch and the simplified version shown in Figure 5, p. 21 is that, instead of a single spring being used, there are a series of strong springs, necessary to hold the flywheel and friction plate in contact. In many cars 'diaphragm' springs are used.

All engines can only operate within a certain range of revolutions per minute. The speed of the wheels of the car, on the other hand, can range from zero up to a very high figure. This is the prime reason why an engine is never directly coupled to the wheels permanently. Instead, a range of gears is provided in order to make the best use of the engine speed. Without a gearbox, the car would have only a much more restricted speed range because the engine would always run at a given number of revs per minute for any given speed. The gearbox, however, enables engine speed to be increased when the car speed is low, thus making use of the torque of the engine. Of course, the gearbox in the modern car is a compromise in which the best selection of gears is provided, taking into account the torque of the engine, the weight of the car, the wheel size, and so on.

If the gearbox and the back axle were coupled together stiffly, the propellor shaft would always be under considerable strain, and fracture would very soon result. For this reason rigid couplings are not used, and universal joints are inserted which enable the shafts to have relative angular movement, thus rendering the drive to the road wheels fairly flexible and so increasing the life of the components. With the rigid type, every time the rear wheels went over a bump the propellor shaft would be subjected to considerable strain, but with the flexible type of coupling the shaft is free to move vertically at its rear end and thus follow the travel of the rear axle when it moves up and down.

We still have a minor problem to overcome. The motion of the propellor shaft, running fore and aft along the line of the car and spinning, must be effectively turned through ninety degrees in order to drive the rear wheels of the car. This is accomplished by the component called the differential (Figure 5) containing the crown wheel and pinion— which are really only names for different types of gear wheels. The basic principle is shown in the sketch. The axle casing which contains the differential assembly must, of course, also incorporate a reservoir for a lubricant, and this lubricant must be of a high quality, because there is an enormous amount of work done in this part of the mechanism. When a car goes round a corner the inner and outer wheels have to turn at different speeds because they are traversing circles with different diameters; suppose the car is 5ft wide, then if the inside wheel is tracing a curve of 25ft diameter, the outside one must obviously be tracing one of 30ft diameter. This necessarily means that the outside wheel will have to travel faster than the inside one. Also inside the differential casing is an ingenious device which overcomes this special difficulty. When the car is travelling in a straight line there would be no tendency for the wheels to move at different speeds, and therefore both halves of the axle (known as half-shafts) would rotate at the same speed. It is sufficient for the novice driver to know and understand that the reason for the differential is to enable the rear wheels to travel at different speeds when necessary. The pinion gear will, of course, always rotate at the average of the two wheel speeds.

The disc wheel was evolved as a result of the spokes of the old-fashioned cartwheel gradually becoming shorter and shorter until they eventually disappeared. The wire wheel is a result of the exact opposite trend, and consists of a large number of spokes arranged at different angles so that their combined tensions enable all the forces due to weight, cornering, braking and drive to be transmitted as evenly as possible between the hub and the rim of the wheel. It is largely used on sporting and high-performance cars today. Wheel change is quick in these cases because there is only one large central nut which has to be dealt with, whereas with the disc wheel there are usually four or five.

There are very many different types and qualities of tyre on the market today, but they all fall into three main groups: cross-ply, radial-ply and bias-belted. These terms merely refer to the method of construction of the tyres. The law now demands that tyres of different types should not be mixed on the same axle. The main advantage of cross-ply tyres is their lower price, and their disadvantage is that the tread is unbraced. If you overload them the centre of the tread does not grip the road surface well, and if you underload them adhesion suffers because only the centre of the tread has an adequate grip. These disadvantages are largely cancelled out by radials, but their price is higher. The bias-belted types combine the best features of the other two, since they have cross-ply walls and a radial type belt under the tread. Tread patterns themselves vary a great deal, from the knobbly 'town and country' type to the asymmetric tread designed to give slow breakaway in fast cornering. A good point to remember if you ever have to mix tyres is 'Radials on the Rear *only*'.

Dunlop's latest effort is a tyre which you can use, when punctured, for up to about a hundred miles at speeds of roughly up to 50 mph. This would seem to be the answer to the motorist's prayer. The secret of this tubeless tyre is that when it deflates, the beads stay put on the rim of the wheel and the tyre collapses upon itself. In doing so, instead of the rim riding over the tyre wall and cutting it so that the rubber gets chewed up, the new tyres ride on a cushion of folded side-wall. Inside, the tyre is provided with a capsule of specially developed lubricant which breaks when the tyre deflates and allows the folds of the wall to slide over each other without damage. This same lubricant also vaporises and slightly inflates the tyre, at the same time sealing off the puncture. It is called a 60 per cent tyre, which means that it is rather wider than it is deep.

When driving fast, however, it is not sufficient to have tyres which grip the road, however excellently; one must also have good brakes in order to bring the car to an early halt if necessary. A travelling car possesses a great deal of kinetic energy, and it has been calculated that when an average car is stopped fairly quickly from about 60 mph, sufficient heat is generated at the brakes to boil a quart of water! This begins to give you an idea of the problem the brakes have to overcome.

Basically there are two types of brake fitted to the modern car: drum brakes (mostly to the rear wheels) and disc brakes (generally to the front wheels). Of course, many cars use drum brakes on all four wheels, or disc brakes on all four (rather less common). Formerly these brakes were worked by means of mechanical linkages, but now the usual method is for the footbrake to operate the front and rear brakes simultaneously by hydraulic means, while the handbrake acts on the rear wheels only by mechanical means. Basically, hydraulic operation means that the pedal causes a piston to be forced against liquid in a cylinder, causing the pressure in the cylinder to rise. This pressure is transmitted along a series of pipes to smaller cylinders located at each wheel.

(Figure 16.) These also have pistons inside them which are forced to move by the changing pressure inside the wheel cylinders, and these pistons force the brake shoes strongly against the brake drum or, in the case of disc brakes, they force the pads against the discs. The reason for hydraulic brakes superseding mechanically operated ones is that piping and hydraulic connections are much simpler to instal and adjust; also the connecting pipes may be run from front to rear of the car inside the bodywork if necessary and so protect the system.

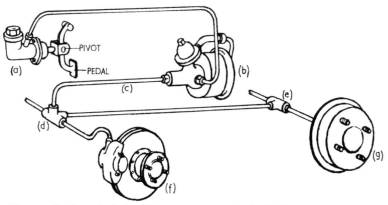

Figure 16   A typical braking system: (a) brake fluid reservoir, which should be kept topped up; (b) 'servo' unit to assist braking power (not found on all cars); (c) brake pipes to conduct fluid to the wheel cylinders (check for corrosion); (d) 4-way junction separating the pipes to each individual system; (e) 3-way junction used to take a fluid feed to the wheel opposite; (f) disc type brake on a front wheel; (g) drum type brake on a rear wheel

When drum brakes get overheated, they are liable to a phenomenon known as fading, which really means that the surface of the brake linings has become polished and shiny, and they are therefore less effective. This is due to the heat acting on the material from which they are made. Disc brakes do not have this particular disadvantage, because the discs are made of metal, and have a relatively large surface area exposed to the outside air, which makes for rapid cooling. Since the front brakes of a car are the ones which are the hardest worked, this is the reason for fitting them on the front wheels. They work in principle just the same as the brakes on a bicycle, except that they grip a specially provided disc instead of the rim of the wheel.

THE ELECTRICAL SYSTEM

The heart of this is the car's battery, for without a battery the car could not be started, nor would it be possible to use lights or horn on a stationary vehicle, much less windscreen wipers, heater or radio etc. Practically all cars today have a twelve-volt installation, which means that your battery has six cells (giving a nominal two volts each), which have to be kept topped up with distilled water. Since all electrical equipment works best when connections are bright and tight, you should make sure there is no corrosion at the terminals of the battery before bothering about the rest of the electrical system. Many a car has failed to start merely because the engine was not getting the message from the battery because its terminals were covered with a horrible greyish green deposit. Moral: keep yours immaculate.

Any electrical circuit requires a 'Go' and a 'Return' path in order to perform its function. In the case of a car, as a general rule, one wire is run to every component which is electrically operated. This is the 'Go' path. The 'Return' path is provided by means of the car body or chassis itself, which of course holds good for a metal-bodied car. Should the vehicle be constructed of fibreglass, for instance, then an artificial 'Return' path will have to be provided to enable the system to work.

If the 'Return' path is electrically poor (say an electrical connection to the body is rusted or corroded) then the component which is most intimately associated with that particular connection will not function. This is often the cause of dim head or side lights, and may be cured by examining all places where connections are made to the body of the car and if necessary removing, cleaning and replacing them tightly.

Obviously a battery has a limited capacity, and so there must be a means of recharging it. This is where the dynamo comes in. This component is usually driven directly from the crankshaft pulley by means of a belt, which should be examined frequently to ensure that it is not sloppy and therefore slipping on the pulley and consequently failing to drive the dynamo and, incidentally, the water pump, which you cannot see. (Figure 17.) The modern tendency is for

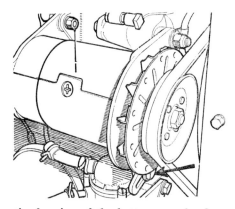

Figure 17 Erratic charging of the battery may be due to a loose fan belt. If so, it can easily be adjusted by loosening the two upper nuts seen in the drawing, moving the component until the fanbelt is at the tension recommended in the driver's manual and securing it in position by means of the bolt (arrowed). Then tighten up the nuts again

manufacturers to provide a small light on the dashboard, usually red, which, when it glows, means the battery is not being charged. As long as it remains out, all is presumably well. This, however, may not always be quite the case. The dynamo could be delivering a low charge; still sufficient to overcome the voltage required to light the bulb, but insufficient to fully charge the battery. This is the reason why keen motorists often fit a meter which will give a direct reading of the rate of charge or discharge of the battery. Such a meter is called an ammeter, and is one of the few 'extras' worth spending money on.

Because the dynamo is an electric machine which needs to be spun at a definite speed in order to produce a worthwhile output, we have to have what is referred to as a 'cutout', also as a voltage regulator, and sometimes loosely as a current regulator—all of which functions it performs. Should this give trouble, it is advisable to have it attended to by a qualified automobile electrician, for he will have the necessary meters and tools for repairing and readjusting it. Fortunately, this particular part of your car is generally pretty reliable and should not give much trouble. As the dynamo has to spin at a certain minimum rate in order to produce a worth-while output, the modern practice is to fit, not a dynamo, but an alternator. This has the big advantage that an appreciable current output is still produced even when the engine is idling in traffic. With the dynamo, if you took your foot off the accelerator pedal, the voltage output dropped accordingly; consequently in consistently dense town traffic the battery was apt to be starved—especially in inclement weather when perhaps all lights were in use together with the windscreen wipers and heater. The alternator, with its correspondingly larger output, can cope with all this.

The golden rule about dealing with electrical matters in cars, if you are not an expert, is: before meddling with anything, disconnect one terminal of the battery. Fuses are provided to protect both battery and components, and incidentally to prevent wiring from overheating and causing a fire. For this reason, if a fuse should fail, do not just replace

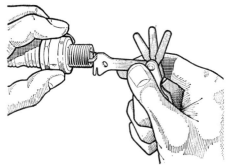

Figure 18 When adjusting the gap on sparking plugs, use the correct tool and bend only the outer electrode. The correct gap is stated in the driver's manual

it with some metallic object like a hairgrip, but try to find out *why* it failed before replacing the fuse. You could thus save yourself a fright and quite a few pounds.

It often helps if you know the colour code for the wiring on your car. Reference to the electrical diagram in the owner's handbook will clear this point up, and a cloth slightly moistened with a mild solvent, such as methylated spirit, will wipe off dirt and enable you to see whether you are tracing the plain blue (headlamp main feed to dipswitch) or the blue with white tracer (headlamp main beam) lead. A standard cable colour coding is used on most British cars.

BODY AND TRIMMINGS

Bodywork on cars has been a sore point with most owners for many years, and is the main cause of cars becoming obsolete. The engines of today are more reliable than the bodies and often outlive them by a number of years, though this state of affairs is now beginning to change as new techniques are adopted by most of the larger manufacturers. Improved derusting processes before painting, better spraying techniques and undersealing methods are at last starting

G   97

to bring in their wake increased body life for the long-suffering owner-driver. It is still necessary to take care of your car's body, though; it cost a great deal of money, and would probably cost even more to replace it. Watch for the slightest chip or crack in the paintwork, often caused by flying stones. If you catch these early enough it is sufficient to touch them in with matching cellulose paint, but if rust—even the slightest trace of it—has begun to rear its ugly head, then it is necessary to rub the affected area down to the bare metal before applying the paint. Use a fine grade of wet and dry paper for this, and 'feather' the edges of the area, so that the repair is not too noticeable.

Make sure when refuelling that no petrol spills on the paintwork. If it does, wipe it off lest it cause a stain, which is unsightly. It is not a good practice to fill your tank right up to the top of the filler pipe, especially in warm weather, because expansion will only cause some of it to be wasted as well as staining the side of the car.

The body and doors are provided with drain holes to allow rainwater and condensation to flow freely away, thus preventing accumulated water from causing rust and corrosion. It is essential that these are kept clear and are not inadvertently blocked.

When carrying out servicing and lubrication of the engine and suspension, get into the habit of making sure that you do not forget to lubricate the door hinges, catches and locks. Bonnet catches are sometimes apt to become dry and cause mysterious squeaks, so do not overlook these.

It is a good idea to place inexpensive rubber mats on the carpets each side of the transmission tunnel in the front seats, since these are the most used seats in the car. This will save excessive wear on the carpets and so enhance the resale value of the car when you come to change it. Besides, these mats can be shaken out regularly; it is much more of a chore to remove and clean carpets, as you will soon find.

CHAPTER EIGHT

Your Driving Test

The Department of the Environment, in their wisdom, recommend that a pupil should have as many lessons with a qualified instructor as is equal to his age in years before thinking of applying for the Driving Test. This sound advice holds good for the average pupil, but I have yet to meet a pupil who considers himself 'average'. Some people (admittedly they are the exceptions) may pass the test after only a few lessons, but on the other hand I remember a dear old lady who had completely filled two record cards. There are spaces for about forty lessons on each card. Older people are naturally somewhat slower to assimilate knowledge and acquire skill with the controls, and in her case the main reason for the slow progress was that she could afford only one lesson a week, and had no car available in which to practise between lessons.

Such practising is all important and once your instructor has pronounced you reasonably safe, it will pay you handsomely to get in as much independent practice between lessons as possible. Sometimes it happens that a woman pupil, after her first effort at practice in the family car, perhaps with her husband, will confide to her instructor that she would much rather drive under the supervision than that of her husband. 'He shouts at me if I do the slightest thing wrong', she will almost sob. If you are a wife or a daughter and it happens to you, don't worry. It only means one of two things. Either you were not quite ready and your instructor had overestimated your confidence, or husband/father/fiancé is being a bit too intolerant.

The reason for intolerance is practically always poor clutch control, and no matter how well you have been doing in the school car, remember that all cars have a different 'point of contact' for the pressure and driven plates of the clutch assembly. This is due to wear, difference in design, varying engineering tolerances, and perhaps even the different ideas of service mechanics when carrying out adjustments. When starting off, therefore, in a different car to the one you have been accustomed to driving, always lift that left foot very gently indeed—even more gently than you have been doing in the school car. This will lead to a smooth start away from the kerb, so that husband/father/big brother gets a very good first impression. Nagging and reprovals will then be much less likely to follow in the event of any subsequent fault.

Learn from this, and resolve to give your examiner a good first impression when you get to the test centre.

Driving tests, whether elementary, commercial or advanced all place the emphasis on safety—*one hundred per cent* safety. There are many instructors (and examiners, too) who regard the present test as anachronistic in view of the increasing traffic density. Pupils, unfortunately, by no means agree with this view. From the time a candidate applies for the test he usually begins to work up a fantastic dread of it. So much so, in fact, that one would imagine he was steeling himself to face a firing squad, or at the very least a major operation, instead of what should be just a pleasant and interesting experience. The examiner is forbidden by law to indulge in violence, no matter how much cause you may give him, so there is really no good reason why anyone should be more scared of him than they are of their dentist. All that the poor chap wants to find out is just how well you can drive, and whether you can be turned loose on the road unaccompanied without becoming a menace to yourself and others.

The Driving Test itself can be described very briefly. Candidates are not asked to do anything really difficult, like parking between two cars at the kerbside or wriggling out of a congested car park when some thoughtless clot has hemmed your car into a corner from which Houdini might find some difficulty in escaping. Nor are they asked to perform any manoeuvres which are more difficult than they have already practised with their instructors.

When you arrive at the test centre, the examiner, whose lot it is to sit beside you for the next half-hour or so, will greet you in a civilised fashion. He will ask you to sign his worksheet against where your name appears, then he will ask to see your licence in order to compare the signature on it with the one you have just put on his sheet. This is merely an attempt to foil any impersonation, but to watch the trembling hands of some people as they hand him their licences— anybody would think the documents were explosive.

Having satisfied himself as far as he is able that you are in fact you, the examiner will ask you to lead him to your car. This is so that he will be able to ask you to read the numberplates on cars other than your own. Once he is satisfied that you do not actually require a white stick, you will be invited to get into the car.

The initial formalities have taken quite a few minutes so far, and it is therefore by no means unusual for only about half an hour or so to be left for the practical part of the test. The examiner's time is scheduled so that each test will take approximately forty-five minutes.

When you both get into the vehicle, the examiner will unobtrusively watch what you do. Don't fiddle. He knows very well that you have driven the car to the test centre, so he will not be impressed at all if he sees you fidgeting with the mirror or the position of the driving seat. These things should already have been adjusted correctly before you drove off in the first place.

Remember, though, to check that the gear lever is in neutral and the handbrake is applied correctly before attempting to start the engine; also to use your mirror and glance over your shoulder before moving off.

The examiner, once you are in the car and before starting the engine, will explain that unless he requests you to turn right or left at junctions, you should go straight on, provided it is safe to do so. After moving off, he will allow you to drive for some distance before asking you to pull in at the side of the road in a position of safety. He will watch for you checking the mirror before signalling your intention to slow down and stop, and when the car has come to rest he will note that you have selected a safe place, ie, one not proscribed by paragraph 97 of the Highway Code, and that your car is parallel to and not too far out from the kerb. All this sounds a lot to remember, but it should not be. If you have been practising regularly, and checking everything you do, it should have become second nature to you by now.

Note the logical nature of the test. The examiner has now satisfied himself that you are able to start and stop the car safely and drive along in a reasonably straight line. He now will ask to you stop as in an emergency when he makes a signal (this usually consists of suddenly smacking the pad on his knee whilst at the same time he says clearly 'Stop'). If you have been watching your rear-view miror as often as you should have been, you will be aware when the road behind is clear and when it is not. The examiner will not ask you to carry out the emergency stop when there is *any* vehicle in the road behind you. The procedure for stopping is quite simple, and should have been explained already by your instructor. All the examiner wishes to see is that you have reasonably normal reactions and that your feet go rapidly and instinctively to the correct pedals. The car should pull up in a straight line without a four-wheel skid, or indeed any kind of skid.

Now comes a little point on which a lot of people fail the test. When you have completed the emergency stop, the examiner will probably say 'Thank you. I will not ask you to do that again'. He will then tell you to move off again when you are ready. It often happens that, overcome by a sense of euphoria after having accomplished a successful emergency stop, people merely drive off again straight away when the examiner speaks. Watch it! What about checking for safety again? Mirror *and* look over shoulder, or failure will be inevitable. It is on such small points that candidates can spoil their chances of a first-time pass.

Only two further manoeuvres remain; the reverse into the side road on the left and the turn in the road. Enough has been said about these in previous chapters, and you will have practised them until you are fairly expert, or your instructor would not have recommended that you apply for the test, so do not worry about the techniques involved. If you cannot do them properly by this time you should not be wasting the examiner's time. One important point, though. Be very careful to check for safety all the time you are carrying out low-speed manoeuvres.

Having now satisfied the examiner that you can perform all these evolutions correctly and safely, your test is almost over except for a short drive in fairly light traffic. If there is a roundabout or traffic lights within easy driving distance of the test centre, you may be assured that he will take you along such a route as will embrace one or both of them. Here again is where your practice pays handsome dividends, because you will already have negotiated them both in the school car and in your own many times and at different times of the day so as to experience a variety of traffic conditions.

Noting your behaviour in traffic and guiding you back to the test centre will conclude the practical portion of the test, leaving only safe parking and, of course, the usual precautions before stopping to be noted by the examiner.

That pad on his knee, by the way, will have been receiving some attention from him intermittently throughout the test. Do not on any account let this worry you. He makes sufficient notes to satisfy himself and also to enable him to complete his report on the test when he gets back into his office. He may also, in the light of your driving technique, decide to ask you certain questions on your return to the test centre, and to remind himself, he will have made notes of these. For instance, suppose on one or more occasions you had driven a little closer to the car in front of you than he personally liked. Obviously one of his questions would then be based upon paragraph 35 of the Highway Code. You might have been perfectly safe on those occasions, or maybe dropped back as soon as you realised you were getting too close. He would wish to satisfy himself that you were, in fact, aware of the provisions of the Code in so far as recommended distances behind other vehicles were concerned. So when you see him writing on that pad, do not worry. It does not necessarily mean that he is noting all your shortcomings. He writes down the good as well as the bad. His questions at the end of the test will be based mainly on the Highway Code and 'related matters', but may also include other more common-sense ones, and perhaps one or two based on the law as it stands on the date of your test.

Just for a moment let us depart from you as the candidate, and consider the examiner for a change. He, poor soul, is expected to sit absolutely still and uncomplaining beside a driver upon whom he has never set eyes until a short while ago. Should the test be taken in a school car, he at least has the dubious comfort of knowing that dual controls are available for his use if necessary. He does not know, though, how many lessons you have had with that particular school, nor how much practice you have had privately between lessons. Always remember, too, both when you are with your instructor and when the examiner is beside you, that there is one thing neither of them can do. That is, to over-ride your brake. Maybe there is an enormous lorry much too close astern, and you are approaching traffic lights. Don't panic. Watch your mirror, and if you have to go across the junction on amber, then tell the examiner why you have done so. He is not a mind reader, and will appreciate whatever justifiable reason you give him for any unusual action such as the one just mentioned. His lot, like Gilbert and Sullivan's policeman, is not a happy one. If the test is being taken in a private car, then the handbrake might perhaps be on the driver's right, and even the ignition switch could be out of reach of the 'qualified driver', who in this case would be highly unlikely to have the blessing of dual controls at his disposal. Examiners, one feels, must wish that all cars were built in the James Bond tradition, with ejector seats and parachutes. And in one widely reported case a few years ago, when a candidate drove car and examiner smartly into a river, even lifebelts would not have come amiss.

It is up to you, therefore, to make him feel as much at his ease as you possibly can right from the moment he enters that potentially lethal vehicle in which you are about to drive him around. Make sure that he sees you checking for safety EVERY TIME you start the engine or move the car off from the kerb, and every time you perform any evolution which is the slightest bit out of the ordinary. Observation—good observation—is the main point which will help you to pass your test. The other great point is smooth driving, by which is meant gentle acceleration, smooth and progressive braking, correct speed on bends and corners, and always being in the correct gear for the speed the car may be doing at any given moment.

Less attention is paid now to arm signals because the DoE have accepted that in modern vehicles most drivers habitually use direction indicators rather than wind down the window to give signals manually. It is possible that your examiner may not require you to make them at all, for the Department consider they have outlived their usefulness. There is, however, one arm signal which will always be valuable—the 'I intend to slow down or stop' signal, which is illustrated in the Highway Code. When preparing to pull in at the side of the road, this signal is considerably less ambiguous than the 'left turn' direction indicator, especially where there may be one or more side roads or entrances on the left. It is therefore the better signal to use in such a case. The other arm signals should still be learned and practised, though, because mechanical indicators can fail, and because arm signals can be necessary for emphasis in certain circumstances. You may use them at your discretion during the Driving Test, and the examiner will judge them in exactly the same way as he judges other aspects of your driving technique.

Now let us suppose that you do not succeed in passing the test the first time. Well, it is not the end of the world, and you will have the opportunity of another month's practice. Make the most of it, so that you will be able to show your examiner next time just how reliable a driver you have become. And in addition to all that extra practice, you will also now know the precise nature of the test. It is really surprising how many people think it is so much more difficult than it really is. And that, coupled with insufficient practice, is often why they fail.

Should your instructor say you are not quite ready for your test, do not disbelieve him. He has nothing to lose whether you pass or fail, but he has a good name to maintain, and it is to his best advantage to prepare you in as few lessons as possible consistent with efficiency. Satisfied pupils are his best advertisement, which is why the most successful instructors are the ones who have least need to advertise their services.

Opinions vary about whether one should take the test at a centre near home or in another district. There are advantages and disadvantages in both cases. If at your local centre, you will be covering familiar ground; though remember that familiarity can also imbue you with a false sense of security. No driver ever thinks he will have an accident in or near the road in which he lives. Perhaps that is why one sees so many of them reversing out of their drives on to a major road at the busiest of times. Do you know ALL the road signs in your area? Are you certain? I once asked a lady driver when approaching a main road junction near a public house only about a quarter of a mile from her own home if she had noticed the sign ahead at her crossroads. 'Of course', she answered, 'it says "Double Diamond Works Wonders," ' whereas if we had been in a district that was strange to her, she would be more likely to have seen the enormous 'STOP' sign together with the double white lines.

Incidentally, do not be too meticulous in answering the examiner's questions at the end of the test—at least not to the extent of another of my ex-victims who, when asked where he would expect to see a Belisha Beacon, replied, quite accurately, 'On top of a black and white pole'.

An appendix at the end of this book gives examples of the kind of question you might possibly be expected to answer. If you can answer every one of them without looking at the specimen answers, then at least your theory is very good, and well up to the standard required for Advanced Driving Tests.

When you have passed your test there is one small point which may save you a few new pence. Look at the expiry date of your provisional licence. If it has more than a month or so to run, it is worth folding that pretty green pass slip the examiner has just given you inside it. That will entitle you to drive away unaccompanied by a qualified driver. You're supposed to be one yourself now!

ADVANCED TESTS

It is possible for anybody who has been properly taught to drive and who religiously puts into practice all the time what he has been taught, to become an Advanced Driver and to pass any or all of the Advanced Driving Tests. Practice, and only practice, gives a person sufficient confidence to handle a car with real skill and that, together with a generous helping of good manners and commonsense, are all that one needs to achieve the highest possible award open to a private driver —the Gold Star of the Car and Motorcycle Drivers' Association.

This book is mainly about elementary driving, but its aim is not only to help you pass your test, but also to become a really good driver in the process. For that reason no apology is offered for the following brief accounts of the three main driving organisations which encourage motorists to further their driving education. They are:

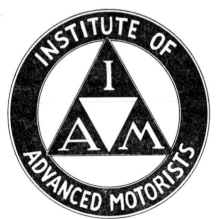

Figure 19   Car badge of the Institute of Advanced Motorists

THE INSTITUTE OF ADVANCED MOTORISTS commenced operations in June 1956, having been formed in order to implement a proposal put forward by the then Minister of Transport. It is a non-profit-making organisation which has as its object: to improve the standard of driving and the promotion of road safety. Applications for Tests should be addressed to The Secretary, The Institute of Advanced Motorists, Empire House, Chiswick High Road, London, W4.

Figure 20   Car badge of the League of Safe Drivers. The colour of the central star-shaped button indicates the member's grade of pass

THE LEAGUE OF SAFE DRIVERS. As with the other organisations, an initial fee covers joining, the first annual subscription and their basic test. Passes, unlike the other organisations, are in three categories and these are distinguished by the colour of the button in the centre of the car badge: gold for Class I, red for Class II and blue for Class III. All grades are fairly high, but Class III is considered just not good enough, and drivers with this class of pass are not allowed to remain members of the League unless they are upgraded at a refresher test at the end of their first year.

Refresher tests are insisted upon at intervals dependent upon one's grade of pass. Queries and membership applications should be sent to The Hon. Secretary, The League of Safe Drivers, Apex House, Grand Arcade, Tally Ho Corner, London, N12.

Figure 21   Car badge of the Car & Motorcycle Drivers' Association, which can be surmounted by a silver or gold star according to the member's qualifications

THE CAR AND MOTORCYCLE DRIVERS' ASSOCIATION was founded by one of the most dedicated of British drivers, the late Ted Lambert, author of a number of motoring books, including *Safe Driving for All*, which has become almost a classic of driving literature. CAMDA, unlike other advanced motoring organisations, runs a carefully graded series of tests, briefly summarised below:

Test 1. A very simple paper which you may complete at home, designed only to jog your memory on the subject of roadcraft. The fee for this is included in the entrance and first year's subscription.

Test 2. This, the Silver Star test, is very similar to the standard tests of the other two advanced driving organisations so far as the road section goes, but is followed by a short written paper which must be completed in the examiner's presence. Successful candidates receive a written report on their driving and are entitled to wear a small silver star over the CAMDA car badge. They also receive the Advanced Driving Licence.

Test 3, the Roadcraft Examination, is an extremely thorough written paper which takes about three hours to complete under supervision. It embraces all aspects of motoring, including driving in adverse conditions, general roadcraft practice, sporting driving and competition work, elementary vehicle maintenance knowledge, and the law in relation to the motorist.

Test 4, the Long Distance Road Test, is a practical driving test over some three hundred-odd miles, during which you have to check in and out at various reporting centres. All candidates finish at a common control, where, after breakfast, a series of driving and manoeuvreability tests are carried out against the clock.

The CAMDA Gold Star, which should be the ultimate ambition of all keen drivers, is awarded to Silver Star holders who have achieved markings in Tests 2 and 3 of at least 70 per cent in each, and the total aggregate of marks in these tests must not be less than 150 out of a possible 200. Marking is very strict, but those who do not quite succeed at their first try can always make more attempts until they eventually succeed.

The Advanced Driving Licence, which is issued by CAMDA to their own Silver Star holders without charge, is also available at a small charge to members of either of the other advanced driving organisations upon proof of their having passed their own version of the Silver Star test. It is a passport-style document containing a photograph of the holder, records details of all tests passed, annual mileage if large enough to be remarkable, continental driving experience, offices held in motoring organisations, writings published on motoring, sporting and competition achievements, and so on. Every claim has to be proved to CAMDA Headquarters and is entered on the licence pages and authenticated by their rubber stamp. Enquiries and applications should be sent to The Administrator, CAMDA, 2 Queensway, Sawston, Cambridge, CB2 4DJ.

Probably because of its impressive title, the most popular Advanced Test by a long way is that of the Institute of Advanced Motorists. The most difficult, and therefore the most challenging, is without doubt the Gold Star of CAMDA. You will not see many Gold Stars about—there are only just over four hundred of them out of the fifteen million-odd private drivers on the roads of Britain today—but this does not mean you cannot become one. At first you may be reluctant to take an advanced driving test, but once you have overcome your disinclination to undergo yet another test, the bug will surely bite, and you will go from strength to strength. And if you ever begin to get dissatisfied with your own standard of driving, that will be the best sign of all. It means that you really do have the makings of a Gold Star driver. Good luck!

APPENDIX

Questions and Answers

The following section may be used as a quiz, or to check your own knowledge of the Highway Code and of roadcraft. If you can answer every question without having to refer to the answers, then your theoretical knowledge is very good indeed.

1 Q. Where might you expect to see green cats' eyes?
A. On a motorway or trunk road verge, where it is joined by a slip road. They mean 'It is safe to cross'. (Don't forget the usual observation, though.)

2 Q. Two cars are approaching each other at crossroads, both wishing to turn right. What is the correct procedure?
A. They should pass offside to offside as a general rule, but this might, in certain circumstances, be impossible, eg, at busy traffic lights, in which case the drivers should be prepared to adapt their techniques to that of the local traffic.

3 Q. In the country you see a 'Cattle Crossing' sign. What specific hazards should you watch for?

A. (a) Cattle, dogs, farm labourers etc emerging from a possibly concealed entrance.
(b) Mud or manure on road, with possible skid risk.

4 Q. What road marking goes with a 'Give Way' sign?
A. A double dotted line signifying the edge of the major road, and possibly an advance warning in the shape of an elongated triangle with its point towards you.

5 Q. You are about to stop your car at the edge of the road on a fairly steep hill. What precautions can you take to prevent it rolling down the hill when you leave it?
A. (a) Set the handbrake.
(b) Leave a low gear engaged (first or reverse, dependent upon whether the car is facing uphill or downhill).
(c) If there is a kerb, turn the wheels in towards it if facing downhill, and outwards if facing uphill.
(d) Make sure also that you have complied with para 97 of the Highway Code.

6 Q. Ahead of you is a white disc with a black diagonal. What does it mean?
A. It means that you have reached the end of the restricted area and may now increase speed provided it is safe to do so. As the law stands in the United Kingdom at the time of writing there are three maximum speed limits on roads which are outside built-up areas; these are:

Motorway .... 70 mph.
Dual Carriageways ...... 60 mph.
Single roads ...... 50 mph.

The definition of a built-up area is one in which the lamp standards are 200yd apart or less, and in these areas speed is normally limited to 30 mph unless the lamp standards carry discs indicating that a higher speed is permitted.

7 Q. Driving along a dual carriageway, you suddenly realise you have just passed the turning you wished to take. What next?
A. Drive on until you reach the next turning. Take it, then retrace your track along the other carriageway until you reach the appropriate turning again.

8 Q. Ahead of you is a car with the red cover of its rear light broken, but the bulb is working. Is the driver committing an offence?
A. Yes. He is not supposed to show a white light to the rear. (See Vehicle Lighting Regulations.)

9 Q. You see fixed to the lampposts at intervals along the road small rectangular green signs with a yellow border and bearing a white letter R. What do they mean?
A. You are on a Ring Road.

10 Q. How fast should you normally drive?
A. At such a speed that you can stop well within the distance you can see to be clear, but this speed must also comply with any restrictions imposed by road signs in the area. (See Q.6.)

11 Q. Entering a strange town, how will you know at once whether you are in a speed-restricted area or not?
A. As a general rule all built-up areas are subject to a 30 mph limit. Those which are not carry appropriate signs fixed to the lamp standards at suitable intervals. The definition of a built-up area is one in which the lamp standards are 200yd apart or less. This may be estimated at about 20 bus-lengths (very approximately).

12 Q. You discover that one or both of your front tyres are wearing unevenly. What action would you take?

A. If neglected, this could lead to a dangerous and possibly illegal state of your tyres. Do not wait for your next service period to come up on the odometer, but take the car to your garage to have the steering geometry checked as soon as possible.

13 Q. It is daytime. Your car is fitted with fog and spot lamps in addition to its standard equipment of lights. Visibility steadily deteriorates and you decide to switch on your lights. Which lights will you use, and why?
A. Dipped headlights, in accordance with para 94 of the Highway Code, because sidelights are almost useless in mist or fog. This recommendation has since been given the force of law by an order making it obligatory for motorists to switch on their headlights in daytime when visibility is poor as the result of fog, snow or heavy rain. The idea is mainly to use your lights so that other traffic can sight you in time and take avoiding action.

14 Q. What is wheelspin?
A. When the driving wheels of the car revolve without gripping the road surface satisfactorily. It is produced by harsh acceleration on a poor surface such as gravel, grass, mud, snow and ice or maybe even fallen leaves in autumn or winter, if they are wet and slippery.

15 Q. What is meant by a white figure '30' on a blue disc?
A. Minimum speed limit is 30 mph. (Don't drop below it.)

16 Q. On a motorway, when is it permissible to overtake on the left?
A. NEVER.

17 Q. Ahead of you is an inverted white triangle with a red border. What, precisely, does this mean?

A. It is a warning that you are approaching a major road junction, and that some short distance ahead will be either a 'GIVE WAY' or a 'STOP' sign. You should therefore reduce speed and approach the junction with caution.

18 Q. What should you do if dazzled by oncoming headlights?
A. Slow down, and stop if necessary.

19 Q. You wish to pull in and stop alongside the kerb to visit a shop, and you see a continuous single yellow line. May you stop?
A. This means that waiting and parking are prohibited during the whole of the working day. The extent of the prohibited time will be defined on a small plate fixed to a lamppost at intervals throughout the prohibited zone. Look at your watch. If you are outside the prohibited times, you may stop. If not, continue, or turn into a relatively quiet side road.

20 Q. With the onset of winter, drivers often fit knobbly tyres of the 'town and country' or 'weathermaster' type. Should you decide to do so, on which wheels of your car would you fit them?
A. On a conventional car they would be fitted to the rear wheels, but on a front-wheel-drive car they would be fitted to the front wheels.

21 Q. Driving along a main road, you wish to take the next turning on the left; there is a driver waiting to emerge from it. How could you show courtesy to him?
A. By making an 'emphasised' left turn signal, ie, an arm signal. If you merely used mechanical indicators, he might possibly think they could have been left flashing

from a previous turn. An arm signal leaves him in no doubt whatever that you really mean to turn.

22 Q. Driving along a fairly wide but winding road, you see ahead a low arched bridge. What action would you take?

A. Since it is a low arched bridge, any high vehicle would have to negotiate it in the middle of the road. Approach with extra caution and keep well over to the left. Use horn (or at night, flash lights).

23 Q. When may you reverse into a major road?
A. Never.

24 Q. Which types of road do you consider to be: (a) the safest; (b) the most dangerous; and why?

A. Without question, those dual carriageways with a central reservation separating them are easily the safest, and the more lanes available on each carriageway, the safer they are. That is why this type of road is used for motorways.

The most dangerous type of road is the three-lane single carriageway type, because the centre lane could be used for traffic overtaking in either direction.

25 Q. Give several reasons for allowing adequate clearance when passing parked vehicles.

A. The door of a parked vehicle may be opened from inside without warning; it may pull away from the kerb without a signal or without its driver checking for safety; pedestrians may emerge suddenly from between parked vehicles; if one is riding a motorcycle or similar vehicle, a parked car may even suddenly disgorge a lighted cigarette-end into one's face as one rides by.

26 Q. You are waiting to emerge from a side road into a major road, and a lorry approaching along the major road gives a short flash with his headlights. What does this mean?

A. It has no official meaning in the Highway Code, and must therefore in itself be ignored. If, however, he is obviously slowing down at the same time, this may be taken as an invitation for you to emerge from the side road if it is safe for you to do so, and if your vehicle has sufficient acceleration for you to pick up speed without inconveniencing other traffic.

27 Q. Where would you expect to see 'safety posts and discs'?

A. These are generally met with in the country, and mark bends and other hazards at the sides of roads. The reflectors on the discs are white on the right of the road and red on the left, so as to be compatible with the lights of vehicles which you would see ahead.

28 Q. You are waiting at a half-barrier type of level crossing, and a train passes. The barriers, however, remain down. How long must you wait before doing something about proceeding, and what would you do?

A. Telephone the signalman from the phone box at the junction after three minutes had elapsed.

29 Q. Your engine suddenly stops while you are stationary at traffic lights at a busy junction. A glance at your gauge shows you are out of petrol. What would you do? You must not hold up other traffic.

A. Put the car in first gear and use that gear to drive the car on the starter across the junction and into the side of the road beyond it so as to clear the junction for other (maybe important) traffic. Always assume that most of the other traffic on the road is more important than your vehicle—it might include an ambulance or a doctor on a life-or-death call. This will not do your starter or battery much good, but provided you do not overdo it, not too much harm should result.

30 Q. On a straight, clear suburban road you are driving along steadily at 30 mph in very light traffic. Suddenly a cat runs out ahead of you. It is impossible to avoid it, and you unfortunately kill it. What do you have to do?
A. Nothing. Drive on. You are not obliged by law to report a cat.

31 Q. A pedestrian steps out in front of your car without looking; you do not have time to make a slowing down signal, but you manage to stop safely. The driver behind is not so fortunate, and he runs into the back of your car, damaging your boot and his radiator. Who is to blame?
A. The driver who ran into the car in front is *always* to blame. (See para 35 of the Highway Code.) This has been repeatedly upheld in courts throughout the land. Get his name and address and the name of his insurance company, and do not forget to try also to get the name and address of the pedestrian as a witness. He may at first be reluctant to oblige, but will probably do so when you explain the situation.

32 Q. On a gantry over a motorway you observe a sign which seems to depict a set of cricket stumps with bails over the left-hand two stumps and nothing over the right-hand one. Meaning?
A. The two left-lanes are closed and only the right-hand lane is at present in use.

33 Q. You are loaned a strange car whilst yours is being serviced. What are the essentials you should check before driving off?

A. First ensure that you are covered by insurance to drive the vehicle, also that, if applicable, it is covered by a current DoE certificate of roadworthiness, and that the Road Fund licence is valid and affixed to the lower left-hand side of the windscreen. Now documentation is correct, so check that the horn, all lights and indicators work correctly. As soon as you move off, wait for a safe moment, then check brakes. Ensure, of course, that you know where the windscreen wiper and washer switches are located and, if it is cold weather, how the heater works. All these checks are best made before actually starting to drive the car seriously. Before doing any long run, make sure you know where the spare wheel is stowed and how to jack up this particular car.

34 Q. Name two places where you would expect to find box junctions.

A. A half-barrier level crossing, and a major road junction controlled by traffic lights.

35 Q. In what respects does a motorway differ from a trunk road?

A. Motorways have signs with blue backgrounds; trunk road signs have green backgrounds. Motorways have hard shoulders, and no right turns; they are always approached by slip roads; they always have telephones spaced regularly for distress calls; no small two-wheelers, agricultural vehicles, animals, pedestrians or L-drivers are allowed, and stopping on the hard shoulder is only permitted in an emergency. Advisory signals at the side of the road should be observed and obeyed, also those on gantries.

36 Q. You pull in at the side of a road correctly and comply with the law in all respects. What is the last thing you should do before getting out of the car?
A. Check the mirror and look over your shoulder before opening the door, and make sure your passengers do not endanger people on the footpath when opening theirs.

37 When stopping at the kerb at night, what does the law require?
A. Choose the left-hand side of the road for stopping, and as soon as the vehicle comes to rest switch off headlights, leaving only parking lights burning.

38 Q. How long may you remain on the hard shoulder of a motorway?
A. Only for sufficient time to deal with whatever emergency caused you to stop upon it.

39 Q. On a three-lane motorway, what is the purpose of each lane?
A. The left-hand lane is for slow traffic such as lorries. The centre lane is for faster traffic. The right-hand lane is for overtaking only, and should not be used except for this. It is normally forbidden for lorries or towing vehicles to use it.

40 Q. On a motorway, where would it be unwise to overtake?
A. High speeds are common on motorways, with resulting strong slipstreams from traffic, and such turbulence is most unpredictable in the vicinity of bridges and similar structures. These could be dangerous spots in which to attempt to overtake, particularly if the overtaken vehicles was a relatively large one.

41 Q. Ahead of you on a motorway is a car towing a caravan. What is his legal speed limit?
A. 50 mph.

42 Q. You are on a side road, approaching a T junction with a major road ahead. It has been snowing heavily during the night, and all signs are covered with snow. How will you be sure whether the signs ahead say 'Stop' or 'Give Way'?
A. A 'Stop' sign is circular, and a 'Give Way' sign is an inverted triangle.

43 Q. What is the accepted meaning of these motoring abbreviations: IFS; FWD; TED; DL 68; MPG; BHP; TDC?
A. IFS = Independent Front Suspension
FWD = Front Wheel Drive (or) Four Wheel Drive
TED = Time exposed to Danger (out of one's own lane)
DL 68 = The DoE booklet *How to pass your Driving Test*
MPG = Miles Per Gallon
BHP = Brake Horsepower
TDC = Top Dead Centre (refers to position of piston in cylinder).

44 Q. What is meant by a 'long wheelbase' vehicle, and what should you watch for when driving behind one of these?
A. Examples of long wheelbase vehicles are articulated lorries, corporation buses, cars towing caravans and so forth. When driving behind one of these, remember it takes relatively longer to pass it, and one must therefore make sure that the road is clear even further ahead than usual before attempting to pull out to overtake. An

even more important point, perhaps, because it is so easily overlooked, is that when a long wheelbase vehicle is turning it takes up much more road room than a normal car or van, and the rear end tends to cut the corner. Motorcyclists have been known to be trapped when attempting to overtake illegally on the inside.

45 Q. At what distance, by law, should you be able to read a car numberplate? If you could just manage to do this, would you be satisfied that your sight was adequate as a driver?
A. 25 yards. No.

46 Q. Apart from 'thinking distance', which of course varies between individuals, what are the main factors which affect your overall stopping distance?
A. Road surface, ie, firm, gravel, muddy, etc.
Weather conditions, ie, ice, snow, rain, fog, etc.
Condition of tyres, ie, depth of tread and tread pattern.
State of brakes, ie, worn or unworn linings and pads.
Distance behind of following traffic.

47 Q. You are in a strange town and at the entrance to a side road you see a white disc with a red border. Meaning?
A. No motor traffic is normally allowed in this road during the times specified on the plate near the sign. It is probably a play street; these are usually closed during the day.

48 Q. What are the three main points of which you should be most aware when reversing into a side road?
A. Careful observation, including checking the road out of which you are reversing before swinging the car's nose

outwards. Fine clutch control to obviate jerkiness. Accuracy.

49 Q. It is illegal to drive with L plates after passing your Driving Test?
A. It is not illegal, but it is rather like crying 'Wolf' too often. If anybody and everybody used L plates just as the mood took them, there would be so many on the road that all drivers would cease to treat cars carrying them with the respect which they are supposed to engender. You can see this for yourself when you spot a private car with L plates and the driver as the sole occupant.

50 Q. At what speed should one overtake other traffic?
A. Having checked ahead and astern, pass as fast as possible in order to reduce the TED, to a minimum, returning to your lane only when you can see the overtaken vehicle in your mirror.

51 Q. What do you know about bus lanes?
A. These are special lanes for the use of buses during periods of rush-hour traffic. They are distinguished by a wider than usual solid white line and during the periods they are in operation no other traffic should use them, except to avoid an accident or to pass obstructions. There is, in addition, a special rectangular blue sign with white lettering carrying the silhouette of a bus and stating the times during which other traffic is forbidden to use the lane. On bus lanes which run in the same direction as the normal traffic on the road, cycles may also be permitted, and where this is the case a silhouette of a cycle will also appear upon the sign. London's Piccadilly is an example of a bus lane which runs contrary to the direction of the normal traffic. The maximum penalty for improper use of a bus lane is £50.

Bibliography

The following books are recommended for further reading:

Driving (the former Ministry of Transport Manual). First published 1969 and reprinted with amendments in March 1970. Available from Her Majesty's Stationery Office and all good booksellers

Sensible Driving, The Logical Basis for Everyday Motoring, by M. J. Hosken (David & Charles, Newton Abbot, 1974)

Steering Clear, by Ted Lambert; The Car and Motorcycle Drivers' Association, 2 Queensway, Sawston, Cambridge CB2 4DJ

Advanced Driving For All, by Ted Lambert; also from the above address

The Lost Causes of Motoring, by Lord Montagu of Beaulieu, available from the National Motor Museum, Beaulieu, Hants, and from all good booksellers

The British Competition Car, by Cyril Posthumous

Cars of the 1930s, by Michael Sedgwick (B. T. Batsford, 1970)

Car Facts and Feats, Edited by Anthony Harding (Guiness Superlatives)

Advanced Motoring, The I.A.M. Manual (Queen Anne Press)

Drink, Drugs and Driving, by A. J. Walls & A. R. Brownlie (Sweet & Maxwell)

The Law for Motorists, a Consumers' Association publication

Owning a Car, a Consumers' Association publication

Milestones in a Motoring Life, by Dudley Noble (Queen Anne Press)

Jackie Stewart's Owner-Driver Book, by Jackie Stewart (Pelham Books)

A Passion for Cars, by Anthony Gibbs (David & Charles, Newton Abbot, 1974)

Index